Sunday, September 7, 2014

Gen 1:26, 24:4, 7, 12-15, 23-27, 36, 40
Gen 24:48-52, 56-58, 61-67
Eph 5:22-32
1 Peter 1:8

God's eternal purpose is to express Himself through a corporate body. (Gen 1:26) He wants us to express Him. These 2 matters are crucial throughout the Bible:
1. dominion and 2. the divine life. No person can express another without their life. God told Abraham's servant to find Isaac a wife. How could that happen? What is the key to all this? Gen 24:7 Abraham was living in oneness with the Lord so He knew what would fill the Lord's desire. I am not there yet. Lord I want to know exactly what you want. Life is the center of Gen 1 & 2 Marriage is the greatest issue in human life. Rebekah was

Crystallization-Study
of
Genesis

Volume Four

Witness Lee

The Holy Word for Morning Revival

Living Stream Ministry
Anaheim, CA • www.lsm.org

First Edition, February 2014.

ISBN 978-0-7363-6833-9

Published by

Living Stream Ministry
2431 W. La Palma Ave., Anaheim, CA 92801 U.S.A.
P. O. Box 2121, Anaheim, CA 92814 U.S.A.

Printed in the United States of America

14 15 16 17 / 5 4 3 2 1

2013 Winter Training

CRYSTALLIZATION-STUDY OF GENESIS

Contents

Preface

1. This book is intended as an aid to believers in developing a daily time of morning revival with the Lord in His word. At the same time, it provides a limited review of the winter training held December 23-28, 2013, in Anaheim, California, on the continuation of the "Crystallization-study of Genesis." Through intimate contact with the Lord in His word, the believers can be constituted with life and truth and thereby equipped to prophesy in the meetings of the church unto the building up of the Body of Christ.

2. The book is divided into weeks. One training message is covered per week. Each week presents first the message outline, followed by six daily portions, a hymn, and then some space for writing. The training outline has been divided into days, corresponding to the six daily portions. Each daily portion covers certain points and begins with a section entitled "Morning Nourishment." This section contains selected verses and a short reading that can provide rich spiritual nourishment through intimate fellowship with the Lord. The "Morning Nourishment" is followed by a section entitled "Today's Reading," a longer portion of ministry related to the day's main points. Each day's portion concludes with a short list of references for further reading and some space for the saints to make notes concerning their spiritual inspiration, enlightenment, and enjoyment to serve as a reminder of what they have received of the Lord that day.

3. The space provided at the end of each week is for composing a short prophecy. This prophecy can be composed by considering all of our daily notes, the "harvest" of our inspirations during the week, and preparing a main point with some sub-points to be spoken in the church meetings for the organic building up of the Body of Christ.

4. Following the last week in this volume, we have provided reading schedules for both the Old and New Testaments in the Recovery Version with footnotes. These schedules are arranged so that one can read through both the Old and

New Testaments of the Recovery Version with footnotes in two years.

5. As a practical aid to the saints' feeding on the Word throughout the day, we have provided verse cards at the end of the volume, which correspond to each day's Scripture reading. These may be cut out and carried along as a source of spiritual enlightenment and nourishment in the saints' daily lives.

6. The content of this book is taken primarily from *Crystallization-study Outlines: Genesis (2)*, the text and footnotes of the Recovery Version of the Bible, selections from the writings of Witness Lee and Watchman Nee, and *Hymns,* all of which are published by Living Stream Ministry.

7. *Crystallization-study Outlines: Genesis (2)* was compiled by Living Stream Ministry from the writings of Witness Lee and Watchman Nee. The outlines, footnotes, and cross-references in the Recovery Version of the Bible are by Witness Lee. Unless otherwise noted, the references cited in this publication are by Witness Lee.

8. For the sake of space, references to *The Collected Works of Watchman Nee* and *The Collected Works of Witness Lee* are abbreviated to *CWWN* and *CWWL,* respectively.

Winter Training
(December 23-28, 2013)

CRYSTALLIZATION-STUDY
OF GENESIS

Banners:

We need to know and experience
the God of Abraham, the God of Isaac,
and the God of Jacob
to become the Israel of God,
the church in the Triune God.

If we would walk in the steps
of Abraham's faith,
we must be those who live the life
of the altar and the tent,
taking Christ as our life
and the church as our living
to live a life of being transfused by God,
consecrating our all to God,
and taking His presence as our road map.

The God of Abraham
is the God of speaking in His appearing,
with calling, in a vision,
and in the human friendship,
to unveil to His intimate friend on the earth
what He aspired for him to be
and what He wanted him to do
according to His heart's desire
for the accomplishment of the eternal
economy for the Divine Trinity.

After we offer to God
what we have received of Him
and what He has wrought into us,
He will return it to us in resurrection,
and we will believe in and experience God
as the God of resurrection
for the fulfillment of His purpose.

Living in Fellowship with God

Scripture Reading: Gen. 18; 2 Chron. 20:7; Isa. 41:8; James 2:23

Day 1   I. "Jehovah appeared to him [Abraham] by the oaks of Mamre as he was sitting at the entrance of his tent in the heat of the day. And he lifted up his eyes and looked, and there were three men standing opposite him. And when he saw them, he ran from the entrance of the tent to meet them" (Gen. 18:1-2):

A. One of these three men was Jehovah God as Christ (vv. 13-14, 22); the other two were angels (v. 22; 19:1).

B. After he was circumcised and his natural strength was terminated, Abraham lived in intimate fellowship with God and became God's friend (2 Chron. 20:7; Isa. 41:8; James 2:23).

II. The glorious intercession that Abraham made before God was not a prayer from man on earth to God in heaven; it was a human, intimate conversation between two friends, an intimate talk according to the unveiling of God's heart's desire (Rom. 4:12; 2 Chron. 20:7; Isa. 41:8; James 2:23; S. S. 1:1-4; Rev. 2:17; Gen. 18; 1 Tim. 2:1, 8):

A. Even before the incarnation (John 1:14) Jehovah as Christ appeared to Abraham in a human form, with a human body, and communed with him on a human level (Gen. 13:18; 18:1-2, 13-15).

Day 2   B. As Abraham was enjoying sweet fellowship with God, he received a revelation from Him regarding the birth of Isaac and the destruction of Sodom (vv. 9-22):

1. The birth of Isaac is related to Christ, and the destruction of Sodom is related to God's judgment upon sin; this means that Christ must come in and that sin must go out.

2. This shows that God's intention is to work Christ into us, to bring Christ forth through us, and to destroy the "Sodom" in our home life, in our work life, and in our Christian and church life (Gal. 1:15-16; 2:20; 4:19; 1 Cor. 5:8).

3. In our intimate fellowship with God, we receive the revelation that all the impossibilities become possibilities with Christ (Gen. 18:14; Luke 18:27).

Day 3   C. God revealed to Abraham His intention to destroy Sodom, because He was seeking an intercessor (Gen. 18:17-22; cf. Heb. 7:25; Isa. 59:16; Ezek. 22:30):

1. While God intended to destroy Sodom, His heart was concerned for Lot, who was dwelling in Sodom (Gen. 13:12; 14:12; 19:1).

2. God wanted to save Lot in order to protect Christ's genealogy through Ruth, a Moabitess and a descendant of Lot (v. 37; Ruth 1:4; Matt. 1:5), but He could not do so without an intercessor.

3. Thus, in His intimate fellowship with Abraham, in a mysterious way, without mentioning Lot's name, God revealed His heart's desire; Abraham's purpose in standing before Jehovah was to intercede for Lot (Gen. 18:22).

Day 4   D. Genesis 18 presents a clear revelation of the basic principles of intercession:

1. The proper intercession is not initiated by man but by God's revelation; thus, the proper intercession expresses God's desire and carries out God's will (vv. 17, 20-21; 19:27-29; Psa. 27:4-8; Heb. 4:16; 7:25; James 5:17).

2. Apparently, Abraham was interceding for Sodom; actually, he was interceding for Lot by implication (Gen. 14:12; 18:23; 19:1, 27-29), showing that we should intercede for God's people who have drifted into the world.

3. Intercession is an intimate conversation with God according to the inward intention of His heart; for this we must learn to linger in the presence of God (18:22-33; Matt. 6:6).
4. Intercession is according to God's righteous way:
   a. In Abraham's intercession for Lot, he did not beg God according to His love and grace; he challenged God according to His righteous way.
   b. God's righteousness binds Him much more than His love and grace do (Gen. 18:23-25; Rom. 1:17).
5. Abraham's intercession did not terminate with Abraham's speaking but with God's, showing that genuine intercession is God's speaking in our speaking (Gen. 18:33; John 15:7; Rom. 8:26-27).

Day 5 **III. To maintain our living in fellowship with God, we need to overcome the stupefying effect of the world's indulgent living (Luke 17:26-32; Gen. 19):**

A. Lot became defeated because he separated himself from Abraham, with whom was God's witness and testimony, and drifted into the wicked city of Sodom (13:5-13; 14:12; 2 Pet. 2:6-9).

B. Ur of Chaldea as a place of idols, Egypt as a place of worldly riches and pleasures, and Sodom as a city of sin form a triangular boundary around the land of Canaan; God's called ones live within this triangle and must be careful lest they fall back to the city of idols, go down to the place of worldly pleasures, or drift into the city of sin (Jer. 2:13; 1 John 5:21; 2 Tim. 3:1-5).

C. In their giving up God, the wicked Sodomites were given up by God to "passions of dishonor"; this is the ultimate issue of man's rebelling against God and rejecting his conscience (Gen. 19:4-11; Rom. 1:21-27; 2:14-15; 1 Tim. 4:2):

1. In God's complete salvation we can be washed from all the sinful things of Sodom, sanctified by God, and justified, accepted, by God (1 Cor. 6:9-11).
2. If we glorify God, thank God, worship God, and serve God, we will be protected from every kind of evil (Rom. 1:21, 25).

Day 6   D. Lot's willingness to sacrifice his two virgin daughters to satisfy the Sodomites' lust shows that Lot, having dwelt a considerable time in the sinful city of Sodom, had lost his sense of morality and shame (Gen. 19:8, 11-13, 30-38):

1. Throughout the whole world the sense of shame and morality has been drugged; because most of the young people were raised in a sinful atmosphere, their senses have been drugged (1 John 5:19).
2. But if they would come into the church life and remain in its pure atmosphere for a few months, they would never return to the sinful world.
3. We all must escape Sodom and shut our doors to its evil atmosphere.

E. Lot had no willingness to escape from the evil and condemned city, but the Lord was merciful, pulling him out of Sodom like wood plucked out of a fire (Gen. 19:16; cf. Zech. 3:2; Jude 19-23).

F. "Remember Lot's wife" is a solemn warning to the world-loving believers (Luke 17:31-32; Gen. 19:15-17, 26; Luke 14:34-35; 1 John 2:27-28).

Morning Nourishment

Gen.   And Jehovah appeared to him [Abraham] by the
18:1-2 oaks of Mamre as he was sitting at the entrance of
       his tent....And he lifted up his eyes and looked, and
       there were three men standing opposite him. And
       when he saw *them,* he ran from the entrance of the
       tent to meet them. And he bowed down to the earth.
16   ...Abraham walked with them to send them away.

One of these three men was Jehovah God (Gen. 18:13-14, 22) as Christ; the other two were angels (v. 22; 19:1). After he was circumcised and his natural strength was terminated, Abraham lived in intimate fellowship with God and became God's friend (James 2:23; 2 Chron. 20:7; Isa. 41:8). Even before the incarnation (John 1:14) Jehovah as Christ appeared to Abraham in human form, with a human body, and communed with him on a human level. (Gen. 18:2, footnote 1)

Today's Reading

What was God's purpose in coming to Abraham in Genesis 18? He surely did not come for a meal; neither did He come to confirm His promise regarding Sarah's giving birth to a son. God came to Abraham because He was seeking an intercessor....The salvation of every Christian has been accomplished through intercession. God did not stay on His throne in heaven waiting for such intercession to occur. Rather, He came down to visit Abraham in the form of a mortal man so that Abraham might easily talk with Him and intercede for Lot. In Genesis 18 Abraham did not pray to God or call on the name of God; he talked to God as with an intimate friend. Thus, the purpose of God's visit to Abraham in this chapter was that Abraham might take up the burden to intercede for Lot according to God's desire.

In order to receive such a revelation from the heart of God, we must pass through a long process. We must come all the way from Ur of Chaldea through many places to the tent door at the oaks of Mamre in Hebron. Firstly God called Abraham by appearing to him as the God of glory. At that time Abraham was neither prepared nor qualified to receive a revelation from God's heart. He was not in intimate fellowship with God. Even after he had slaughtered Chedorlaomer and the other kings, Abraham was not ready to converse with God in an intimate way. In chapters 15 and 16 we see that although Abraham was a man who sought God and loved Him, he was still so much in his flesh. In chapter 17 he was circumcised and terminated, his name was changed from Abram to Abraham, and he became another person. Then, in chapter 18 God came to him at the oaks of Mamre in Hebron not as the God of glory nor as the Most High God, the Possessor of heaven and earth, nor as the El-Shaddai, but as a mortal man to enjoy a meal with His intimate friend. At that time God had found a man who was after His heart. The glorious intercession which Abraham made before God in Genesis 18 was not a prayer from man on earth to God in heaven; it was a human conversation between two friends. God came down from heaven, lowering Himself, putting on the form of a mortal man, and conversing with Abraham. Eventually, He indicated to Abraham that He was the Almighty God; yet they continued to talk as two friends. When Abraham was in this condition, he was prepared and qualified to receive a revelation from God's heart concerning His desire. Intercession is an intimate talk with God according to the unveiling of His heart's desire. (*Life-study of Genesis,* pp. 678-681)

The Bible says that Abraham was the friend of God. In Genesis 18 the God of heaven came to earth in order to befriend Abraham. Both the Old Testament and the New Testament say that Abraham was a friend of God (2 Chron. 20:7; Isa. 41:8; James 2:23). Our impression of God is that [since] He is too great and that we are so low…it must not be easy to converse with Him, draw near to Him, pray to Him, or even cry out to Him….Very few know that we can pray to God just as we speak with other human beings. (*The Meaning and Purpose of Prayer,* pp. 19-20)

Further Reading: Life-study of Genesis, msg. 51

Enlightenment and inspiration: _____
_____
_____
_____

Morning Nourishment

Gen. **Is anything too marvelous for Jehovah? At the**
18:14 **appointed time I will return to you, according to**
the time of life, and Sarah shall have a son.
20 **And Jehovah said, The cry of Sodom and Gomorrah,**
how great it is; and their sin, how very heavy it is!

As Abraham was enjoying such sweet fellowship with God, he received revelation from Him regarding the birth of Isaac and the destruction of Sodom. These are the two basic things concerning which God will always deal with us. The birth of Isaac is related to Christ, and the destruction of Sodom is related to God's judgment upon sin. Isaac must come and Sodom must go. This means that Christ must come in and sin must go out.... God's concern is to bring Christ forth through us and to eliminate all the sinful things. He intends to produce Christ and to destroy the "Sodom" in our home life, work life, and even in our Christian and church life. (*Life-study of Genesis*, p. 673)

Today's Reading

All the revelation that we have received and shall receive from God mostly concerns these two items. If you consider your own experience, you will find that this is so. Whenever you have received revelation from God during the course of your fellowship with Him, it has always concerned Christ on the positive side and sin on the negative side. Positively we see more of Christ and say, "I have seen something new of Christ. How I hate that I have not lived more by Him." This is the revelation regarding the birth of Isaac, the revelation that Christ will be brought forth in your life. But negatively we see our sins and say, "O Lord, forgive me. There is still so much selfishness, hatred, and jealousy in me. I have so many failures, shortcomings, and even sinful things. Lord, I judge these things and want them destroyed." This, in principle, is God's judgment upon and destruction of sin. In our Christian life, Christ must be brought in and "Sodom" must be destroyed. Likewise, in the church life, Christ must increase and sin must be abolished.

How can Christ be brought forth? Firstly, there is the promise. The promise made to Abraham regarding the birth of Isaac in Genesis 17:19 and 21 was confirmed in 18:10. Not only did God promise Abraham that he would give birth to Isaac through Sarah, but in the whole Bible, especially in the New Testament, there is the rich promise concerning Christ. We have the promise that Christ will be our life, our supply, and our everything. How much the New Testament promises concerning Christ! All these promises can be fulfilled by the gracious visitation of God.

The birth of Isaac was at the time of life, at the appointed time (17:21; 18:10, 14). Christ always has been and always will be increased in us and brought forth through us at the time of life. We need to have many such times of life.…The time of life is always the appointed time, the time appointed by God. God made the appointment, not Abraham. It is the same with us today, for it is God who makes the appointments, not you and I.… Whenever God comes to visit us to bring forth Christ, that time is the appointed time, the time of life.

The time of life for Abraham and Sarah was the time when they had become nothing. Isaac was born when Abraham had become as old as dead and Sarah had become out of function (vv. 11-13). Likewise, whenever we become nothing, that is a good time, a divinely appointed time, for us to participate in more life.

In verse 14 the Lord said, "Is anything too marvelous [or wonderful] for Jehovah?" Every experience of Christ is marvelous in our eyes; it is a wonderful doing of the Lord. How could Sarah have brought forth Isaac? It was humanly impossible. If that had happened to us, it would have been a wonderful and marvelous thing in our eyes. Christian experiences are always like this because the Christian life is a life of impossibilities. How marvelous it is that all the impossibilities become possibilities with Christ! (*Life-study of Genesis,* pp. 673-675)

Further Reading: Life-study of Genesis, msg. 50

Enlightenment and inspiration: _____

_____

_____

_____

Morning Nourishment

Gen. **And Jehovah said, Shall I hide from Abraham what**
18:17 **I am about to do?**
   22 **And the men turned from there and went toward**
      Sodom, while Abraham remained standing before
      Jehovah.

God revealed to Abraham His intention to destroy Sodom, because He was seeking an intercessor. While God intended to destroy Sodom, His heart was concerned for Lot, who was dwelling in Sodom (Gen. 13:12; 14:12; 19:1). He wanted to save Lot in order to protect Christ's genealogy through Ruth, a Moabitess and a descendant of Lot (19:37; Ruth 1:4; Matt. 1:5), but He could not do so without an intercessor. Thus, in His intimate fellowship with Abraham, in a mysterious way, without mentioning Lot's name, God revealed His heart's desire. The proper intercession is not initiated by man but by God's revelation. Thus, it expresses God's desire and paves the way for the accomplishing of His will. (Gen. 18:17, footnote 1)

Abraham's purpose in standing before Jehovah was to intercede for Lot. The glorious intercession that Abraham made before God was not a prayer from man on earth to God in heaven; it was a human conversation between two friends, an intimate talk according to the unveiling of God's heart's desire. (Gen. 18:22, footnote 1)

Today's Reading

On His throne in heaven, God had decided to execute His judgment on the wicked city of Sodom. But God would never forget that one of His people, Lot, was in that city. Lot did not even realize that he had to be rescued from Sodom. What could God do? He had to find someone to intercede for Lot. God knew that there was no one on earth who was as concerned for Lot and who was so much with God as Abraham was. Hence, God came to Abraham for the purpose of finding an intercessor. Without an intercessor to intercede for His people, God cannot do anything. God has His divine principles. One of them is that without intercession He cannot save anyone.

As Abraham lingered in God's presence, even after the two angels had left for Sodom, remaining standing before Him (Gen. 18:22), God opened up to him. God did not open to Abraham directly but in the way of implication. God did not say, "Abraham, I shall soon destroy Sodom. Lot is there, and I am very concerned about him. I have come to ask you to intercede for him." God was not that simple. Instead, He said, "The cry of Sodom and Gomorrah, how great it is; and their sin, how heavy it is! I shall go down and see whether they have done altogether according to its outcry, which has come to Me; and if not, I will know" (18:20-21). Although God did not say a word about Lot, His intention in speaking about Sodom was for Lot. These two friends talked about Lot, but neither of them mentioned his name. They spoke about him in a mysterious way, in a way of implication....Nevertheless, God knew Abraham's intention as Abraham knew God's intention. (*Life-study of Genesis,* pp. 678-680)

Before God saves, edifies, or works in someone, He must find a person to pray for the things that He is about to do. Without our prayer, God cannot work. God visited Abraham so that Abraham would intercede for Lot to be saved. It is possible to say that God was asking Abraham to do something; hence, it was not easy for God to bring it up. It is easy to tell a person what we will do for him, but it is not easy to ask someone to do something for us. God wanted Abraham to do something, but in order to see if Abraham was willing, He did not bring it up quickly. If I want to ask a brother to help me, I would first talk with him to see how his heart is toward me. Only if he cares for me would I feel comfortable asking him to help me. This was the case when God spoke with Abraham. It was when Abraham walked with God to send God off and lingered in God's presence that God said, "Shall I hide from Abraham what I am about to do?" (Gen. 18:17). (*The Meaning and Purpose of Prayer,* p. 22)

Further Reading: The Meaning and Purpose of Prayer, ch. 2

Enlightenment and inspiration: _____

_____

_____

Morning Nourishment

Gen. Far be it from You to do such a thing, to put to
18:25 death the righteous with the wicked, so that the
      righteous should be as the wicked. Far be it from
      You! Shall the Judge of all the earth not do justly?
   33 And Jehovah went away as soon as He had finished
      speaking with Abraham, and Abraham returned
      to his place.

The only intercession that counts in the eyes of God is that
which is according to His revelation. This means that proper
intercession is not initiated by us but by God in His revelation.
    In order to fulfill the first basic principle of intercession...
we need to pass through a long process. We need to be dealt
with, circumcised, and terminated. Then we shall be ready for
intimate fellowship with God. God will come to us on a human
level, not on a divine level, just as He came to Abraham...[so
that he could speak] with Him face to face. How good it is to talk
with God in this way! When we have fellowship with God like
this, we do not have the sense that we are talking to the
almighty, majestic God, but to another human being. This is
the meaning of intercession being according to the revelation of
God. This intercession is always intimate, mysterious, and in
the way of implication. (*Life-study of Genesis,* pp. 677, 681)

Today's Reading

Since all proper intercession is according to the revelation
which is out of God's heart, it must also be according to God's
heart....Although God did not mention Lot by name, Abraham
realized what was on God's heart. Abraham did not intercede
according to the outward word of God but according to the
inward intention of God's heart. Proper intercession must always touch the heart of God.
    In Genesis 18 Abraham was not praying; he was talking to
his intimate Friend on a human level....When you have come
into intimate fellowship with God on the human level and
know His heart's desire, you can challenge Him, saying, "Lord,

is this Your way?" This is neither praying nor begging; it is challenging God in a very friendly conversation.

Abraham's challenge to God was according to God's righteous way (18:23-25)....Proper intercession is neither according to God's love nor according to His grace, but according to His righteousness....We must challenge God according to His righteousness because His righteousness binds Him more than His love and His grace do. God has no obligation to be loving or to show grace, but He is held responsible to be righteous.... Proper intercession never begs God according to His love but challenges Him according to His righteous way.

Abraham's intercession echoed the desire of God's heart concerning Lot. As he was interceding according to God's heart, his intercession spontaneously expressed God's desire....This is another principle of intercession.

Intercession must also carry out God's will. Although God had a will to rescue Lot, without Abraham's intercession God had no way to carry out His will. Proper intercession always paves the way for the accomplishing of God's will. It lays the tracks for the heavenly locomotive. God desired to rescue Lot from Sodom, but He had to find a way to do this. Thus, He visited Abraham for the purpose that he might intercede on Lot's behalf. Abraham was intimately close to God's heart, and God was able to open His heart to him. Immediately Abraham echoed back to God His heart's desire in a challenging intercession.

This chapter does not end with Abraham's speaking; it ends with God's speaking [v. 33]....It does not say that Abraham had finished his speaking; it says that the Lord had finished His speaking. Proper intercession is always God's speaking. Apparently we are speaking; actually God is speaking in our speaking....We need to stay in the presence of God until He has finished His speaking to us. Our intercession must utter what God is speaking. (*Life-study of Genesis,* pp. 682-683, 685-688)

Further Reading: Life-study of Genesis, msg. 51

Enlightenment and inspiration: _____

_____

_____

_____

Morning Nourishment

Gen. Abram dwelt in the land of Canaan, and Lot dwelt
13:12 in the cities of the plain and moved his tent as far
as Sodom.

19:1 And the two angels came to Sodom in the evening,
and Lot was sitting in the gate of Sodom. And
when Lot saw *them*, he rose up to meet them and
bowed with his face to the ground.

Lot was a righteous and godly man (2 Pet. 2:6-9). Nevertheless, although he had come out of Ur of Chaldea and was dwelling
as one of God's people with Abraham in the land of Canaan (Gen.
12:5), he became defeated because he separated himself from
Abraham, with whom was God's witness and testimony, and
drifted into the wicked city of Sodom (13:11-13; 14:12), which was
condemned by God and was to be destroyed under His judgment.

Ur of Chaldea was a place of idols, Egypt was a place of worldly
riches and pleasures, and Sodom was a city of sin. These three
places form a triangular boundary around the land of Canaan.
God's called ones live within this triangle and must be careful lest
they fall back to the city of idols, go down to the place of worldly
pleasures, or drift into the city of sin. (Gen. 19:1, footnote 1)

Today's Reading

The Bible does not indicate that in the strife between Lot and
Abraham in Genesis 13 Abraham was wrong. However, I believe
that in a very deep sense Lot's feelings were hurt. Here I would
say a word to the leading brothers. It is a very difficult matter to
deal with the brothers. Abraham did nothing wrong in dealing
with Lot, but simply because he dealt with him, Lot would never
return to him. Abraham never forgot Lot. When he heard that Lot
had been captured by Chedorlaomer, he led the fight against the
kings and rescued Lot. When Abraham learned that God was
about to destroy Sodom, he interceded for Lot. In 19:27 and 28,
Abraham rose up early in the morning and looked toward Sodom
and Gomorrah because he was so concerned for Lot. Nevertheless, because of his hurt feelings, Lot would not return to

WEEK 19 — DAY 5

Abraham....When Lot was delivered from the city of Sodom, he did not consider returning to Abraham. If he had returned, his life would not have had such a pitiful ending.

I am burdened that the young brothers and sisters will see that it is dangerous to dissent with and to leave the older generation in the Lord....There is no indication in the Word that Lot thanked Abraham for delivering him from captivity. It might have been that he would not give up his hurt feelings and humble himself. We should not insist upon holding on to such human feelings. We, unlike Lot, should humble ourselves, lose our face, and return to Abraham and remain with him. The sooner we do this and the more we do it, the better.

Lot drifted into a situation which was wicked and sinful before God (13:11-12). Once you leave the source of spiritual influence, you will automatically go downhill....Never forsake the proper spiritual influence, for it is your protection. If you give it up, you will lose your protection, and, like Lot, will drift downward into Sodom. In spite of the fact that Lot knew Sodom was wicked in the eyes of God, he eventually entered into that evil place and lived there....When the two angels came to execute God's judgment over Sodom, Lot was sitting in the gate of the city, in contrast to Abraham who was sitting at his tent door. According to ancient custom, whoever sat at the gate of the city was one of the elders, for only they had the privilege of sitting there. Lot became a leader in Sodom! (*Life-study of Genesis,* pp. 692-695)

Although we all are saved and are living somewhere in Romans 5 through 8, we still need to know the source of evil and the way to be restricted from doing evil....We need to know God by His creation and hold His truth in righteousness. We need to act according to our nature, heed the voice of our conscience, and care for the proper reasonings within us. If we practice all these things, we will be protected. (*Life-study of Romans,* p. 39)

Further Reading: Life-study of Romans, msg. 3; *Life-study of Genesis,* msg. 52

Enlightenment and inspiration: _____

_____

_____

_____

Morning Nourishment

Gen. **But he lingered; so the men seized his hand and**
19:16-17 **the hand of his wife and the hand of his two daugh-**
ters, Jehovah being merciful to him, and they
brought him out and set him outside the city. And
when they had brought them outside, He said,
Escape for your life. Do not look behind you....
Escape to the hills, lest you be destroyed.
Luke **Remember Lot's wife.**
17:32

Lot's wife became a pillar of salt because she took a lingering look backward at Sodom, indicating that she loved and treasured the evil world that God was going to judge and utterly destroy. She was rescued from Sodom, but she did not reach the safe place that Lot reached (Gen. 19:15-30). She did not perish; neither was she fully saved. Like the salt that becomes tasteless (Luke 14:34-35 and footnote 2 on verse 34), she was left in a place of shame. This is a solemn warning to the world-loving believers. (Luke 17:32, footnote 1)

Today's Reading

While the angels were staying in Lot's house, the Sodomites came to indulge in their sodomitical lust, coming from every corner of the city (Gen. 19:4-11). A Sodomite is a homosexual. Paul speaks of them in Romans 1:24 and 27. There are many Sodomites today and much sodomitical lust is expressed. Sodomites seem to have no spirit; they are like brutal animals.

Lot was even willing to sacrifice his two daughters to satisfy the Sodomites' lust (Gen. 19:7-9). Whether he was forced to do this or not, he never should have done it. This shows that Lot's sense of morality had been drugged....Lot would consider sacrificing his virgin daughters to save his two guests....Although he was a righteous man, he had lost his sense of morality and shame.

To meet such a wicked situation, the angels smote the Sodomites with blindness (19:11), indicating that all the men in Sodom were blind and in darkness....If a man were not blind, how could he be a Sodomite? This shows that sinfulness blinds people.

Others of Lot's children had no sense of morality (19:30-35)....
After escaping from Sodom, Lot and his daughters still had wine
with them (19:32). If they had not brought the wine with them,
how else could they have had it in the cave where they were
dwelling? How drugged they were by the sinful situation in
Sodom!...For young ladies to be without a sense of shame is to be
without protection. Throughout the whole world the sense of
shame and morality has been drugged. Because most of the
young people were raised in a sinful atmosphere, their senses
have been drugged. But if they would come in to the church life
and remain in its pure atmosphere for a few months, they would
never return to the sinful world.

We live in an evil age and need protection from it. Our family
and our children must be protected. We all must escape Sodom
and shut our doors to its evil atmosphere. If we do not, our
descendants will be drugged. How could Lot and his children
have conducted themselves in the way they did after Sodom was
destroyed? Because their sense of morality had fallen so low.

Lot himself was barely saved through the overcomer's intercession (19:15-25, 29). Even after the angels told Lot that Sodom
was to be destroyed, he still lingered there. He had no willingness to escape from the city, but the angels held his hand and
pulled him out [v. 16]....Lot was not faithful, but the Lord was
merciful, pulling him out of Sodom as wood plucked out of a fire.

In Luke 17:28-33 the Lord warns us not to look back. Why did
Lot's wife look back? Because some of her children, especially
her daughters, were still in Sodom and because her house and her
clothing also were there. If you read Genesis 19 carefully, you will
see that she was behind Lot....Being behind him, she looked
back and became a pillar of salt....When the day of judgment
arrives, will you share in the glory or in the shame? We shall not
suffer perdition, for our salvation is assured. However,...we may
be put to shame. (*Life-study of Genesis,* pp. 695-698)

Further Reading: Life-study of Genesis, msg. 53

Enlightenment and inspiration: _____

_____

_____

_____

Hymns, #485

1   What great provision God has made
    In Jesus' death on Calvary!
    I hung with Him upon the tree,
    And in His tomb I too was laid.

2   I rose with Him from out the grave—
    And how shall I who died to sin
    Continue still to live therein,
    The victor living as the slave?

3   At God's right hand He took His place,
    And while for saints my Savior pleads,
    My heart for sinners intercedes
    That they might know His saving grace.

4   Oh, what a name to me is given—
    A son of God, by second birth!
    I represent Him on the earth,
    He represents me now in heaven.

5   As Jesus dwells beyond the skies,
    I dwell within this world of strife;
    And as He lives within my life,
    In Him I'm in the heavenlies!

Composition for prophecy with main point and sub-points: _____

The God of Abraham Seen
in His Dealings with Abraham

Scripture Reading: Acts 7:2; Gen. 12:7-8; 13:14-17; 14:17-20; 15:1; 17:1; 18:1; 24:14

Day 1   **I. The God of Abraham (Exo. 3:15) is seen in His dealings with Abraham as follows:**

A. The God of Abraham is the God of glory, in His first appearing with His first calling and His first speaking to Abraham, as the vast magnet and the great motivation to Abraham that moved him to come out of the country of satanic idolatry (Gen. 11:31; Acts 7:2-4a):

1. Through His repeated appearing to Abraham, God transfused Himself into him, causing him to experience a spiritual infusion (Gen. 12:1-3, 7-8; 13:14-17; 15:1-7; Rom. 4:3; Gen. 18:17-19; cf. Acts 26:16; 22:14-15).

2. Abraham was able to reach Canaan because God was persistent; God holds His people fast; He is a God who will not let go (John 10:28-30; Jude 24).

3. God was revealed to Abraham as the Justifier of His believing people who have been transfused with Him as their believing element to be their faith, which is their appreciation of Him as a divine reaction to His attraction (Gen. 15:1-6; Heb. 12:1-2a; Gal. 2:20).

Day 2   B. The God of Abraham is the God of blessing, in His second calling with His second speaking to Abraham, promising him that He would make of him a great country, make his name great, and make him a blessing to others and that all the families of the earth would be blessed in him; this attracted Abraham to go into the good land of the divine promise (Gen. 12:1-4):

1. According to Galatians 3:14, the blessing promised here is actually God Himself as the Spirit; the greatest blessing is the Triune God—the Father, Son, and Spirit—as the processed, all-inclusive, life-giving Spirit dwelling in us in a most subjective way for our enjoyment (6:18; Phil. 1:19).
2. Whoever curses God's people receives a curse, and whoever blesses God's people receives a blessing (Num. 23:21; 24:5, 9; cf. 1 Cor. 1:2; 2 Cor. 5:17).

Day 3   C. The God of Abraham is the God of the earth, in His second appearing with His third speaking, in promising Abraham that He would give the land of Canaan to his seed (Gen. 12:6-7).

D. The God of Abraham is the God of secret care for His elect, in saving Abraham from Pharaoh's insulting of his wife (vv. 10-20).

E. The God of Abraham is the God of comfort and encouragement, in His fourth speaking, after Lot left Abraham, in promising to give to Abraham and to his seed the land of Canaan as far as he could see in four directions and to make his seed as numerous as the dust of the earth (13:14-17):
1. Christ as the seed of Abraham must be wrought into us so that He may be brought forth through us for His increase (Gal. 3:16; 1:15-16; 2:20; 4:19).
2. The land of Canaan signifies the all-inclusive Christ as the all-inclusive Spirit in our spirit for our enjoyment so that we may be constituted with Him for His corporate expression (Col. 1:12; 2:6-7; Gal. 3:14; 5:16, 25).

F. The God of Abraham is God the Most High, Possessor of heaven and earth, in His divine supply with His blessing to Abraham through His priest Melchizedek after Abraham fought the battle against the four kings (Gen. 14:17-20).

Day 4

    G. The God of Abraham is the God of shield and great reward, in His fifth speaking (this time in a vision) to Abraham, when he was afraid of the four kings' avenging, in pointing out to Abraham that his heavenly seed in their divine nature would be as many as the stars in heaven who could never be touched by anyone on earth; Abraham believed in Jehovah, and Jehovah accounted it to him as righteousness (15:1-6).

    H. The God of Abraham is the God of faithfulness, in foretelling to Abraham, in His sixth speaking to him in his deep sleep, that his earthly seed in their human nature would be sojourners in Egypt, serve the Egyptians, be afflicted by them for four hundred years, and in their fourth generation return to Canaan; and He is the God of faithfulness, in making a covenant with him that He would give to his seed the land from the river of Egypt to the Great River, Euphrates (vv. 12-21).

    I. The God of Abraham is the God of silence, due to the fact that Abraham listened to his wife Sarah and married Hagar to get a son by the exercise of his flesh when he was eighty-six years old (16:1-4, 15-16); then God became silent to Abraham for thirteen years, until he became ninety-nine years old, and God appeared to him again (17:1).

Day 5

    J. The God of Abraham is the God of all-sufficiency, in His third appearing with His seventh speaking to Abraham, in being the God of circumcision to cut off His chosen people's natural man in the flesh that they may become God's new creation, signified by Isaac who was born by God's grace, not by Ishmael who was born by Abraham's flesh (vv. 1-21; Gal. 4:22-31):

        1. God is revealed as the All-sufficient God (Heb. *El Shaddai*) for His believing ones to walk in His presence, constantly enjoying

Him and His all-sufficient supply, and to
have God added to them as the element and
factor of their perfection (Gen. 17:1).

2. The divine title *El Shaddai* is composed of
two Hebrew words—*El* means "the Mighty
One," and *Shaddai* comes from the Hebrew
word meaning "breast" or "udder."

3. Thus, God is the Mighty One with an udder,
the all-sufficient Mighty One to be the Nour-
isher, Strength-giver, and bountiful Supplier
of His called ones, who continually receive
Him (Phil. 1:19-21a; Gal. 3:2, 5; John 1:16).

4. The All-sufficient God is the God of crucifixion for the termination of our natural man in
the flesh and the God of resurrection for the
germination of our new man for the new creation (Gen. 17:1-21; 22:1-10; Col. 2:11; Gal.
5:24; 1 Pet. 1:3; 2 Cor. 5:17; Phil. 3:3).

K. The God of Abraham is the God with His human
friendship, in His coming (in His fourth appearing with His eighth speaking to Abraham) as a
man, in the form of a man, to visit Abraham as
His friend (2 Chron. 20:7; Isa. 41:8; James 2:23)
on the level of humanity, with whom Abraham
walked and who conversed with Abraham as a
human friend with a human friend, concerning
His judgment of Sodom, where His friend's nephew Lot and his family lived (Gen. 18—19).

L. The God of Abraham is the God with friendship
in humanity, in sending Abraham's nephew and
his two daughters out from the overthrow of
Sodom, for the remembrance of Abraham as His
intimate friend (vv. 29, 12-22).

Day 6 M. The God of Abraham is the almighty God with
His friendly care, in saving His close friend Abraham, with His almighty power, from the loss of
his wife to Abimelech, king of Gerar (ch. 20).

N. The God of Abraham is the God of changelessness in keeping the principle of His grace, in

recognizing Isaac, his son of Sarah, as his only
son, in His ninth speaking to Abraham (21:1-12).
O. The God of Abraham is the God with His trial, in
proving Abraham, His intimate human friend,
by asking him to present his only son, whom he
loved, for a burnt offering to Him, in His tenth
speaking to Abraham (22:1-10).
P. The God of Abraham is the Triune God of provision (Heb. *Jehovah-jireh*), in His providing a ram
to replace Isaac for a burnt offering to Him (as
the Angel of Jehovah—Christ), in His eleventh
speaking to Abraham (vv. 11-14).
Q. The God of Abraham is the Triune God of blessing, in His twelfth (last) speaking to Abraham,
promising him that He (as the Angel of Jehovah—Christ) would bless him and multiply his
seed like the stars of the heavens and like the
sand upon the seashore and that in his seed
(Christ) would all the nations of the earth be
blessed (vv. 15-18).
R. The God of Abraham is the God of friendship on
the human level, in leading the old servant of
His friend Abraham to secure a wife for his son
Isaac (ch. 24).
II. As a whole, the God of Abraham is the God of
speaking in His appearing, with calling, in a
vision, and in the human friendship, to unveil to His intimate friend on the earth what
He aspired for him to be and what He wanted
him to do according to His heart's desire for
the accomplishment of the eternal economy
for the Divine Trinity.

Morning Nourishment

Acts ...The God of glory appeared to our father Abra-
7:2-4 ham while he was in Mesopotamia, before he dwelt
in Haran, and said to him, "Come out from your
land and from your relatives, and come into the
land which I will show you." Then he came forth
from the land of the Chaldeans and dwelt in Haran.
And from there, after his father died, He removed
him into this land, in which you now dwell.

In Exodus 3:15 God declared that He is the God of Abraham,
but without any details. It was in so many dealings of God with
Abraham that the details of what God is were unveiled.

The God of Abraham is the God of glory. Stephen told us that
when Abraham was called by God in Ur of the Chaldees, God
appeared to him in glory as the God of glory (Acts 7:2-4a). God's
glory is God Himself expressed. If God hides Himself, there is
no glory. If God appears, if God is expressed, that is glory. God's
glory in His appearance might imply a kind of splendor, bright
and shining. (*The History of God in His Union with Man*, p. 93)

Today's Reading

The God of glory in His first appearing to Abraham with His
first calling and His first speaking was as a vast magnet and
great motivation to Abraham, which moved him to come out of
the country of satanic idolatry (Gen. 11:31).

Abraham was attracted, but Genesis shows us that he did
not answer God's call in an absolute and willing way. It was not
Abraham that took the lead to initiate leaving the world of idolatry. His father took the lead, and he followed. Actually, though,
God was the magnet and motivation which moved Abraham to
come out of the country of satanic idolatry. Abraham would not
have made this move if God had not come to him as the God of
glory. (*The History of God in His Union with Man*, p. 93)

When a person has been called by God in this way, the living
God transfuses Himself into him. This word *transfuse* is important
in describing what transpires at God's calling. The living God

spontaneously transfuses Himself into the called one. As a result, he is attracted by God and to God. Unconsciously, some element, some essence of the living God is transfused into him, and he reacts to God by believing in Him. This reaction is faith.

Many of us have held the wrong concept about Abraham… that he was a giant in faith,…[but] the only giant of faith is God Himself. God, as the giant of faith, transfused Himself into him. After Abraham had spent time in God's presence, he could not help believing in Him, because he had been transfused with God. Thus, Abraham was attracted to God and reacted to Him in believing. His reaction was his believing.

The first appearing was that recorded in Acts 7. Two more appearings are found in Genesis 12: in the first of these (vv. 1-3) God told Abraham to leave his country, his kindred, and his father's house; in the second one (vv. 7-8) God promised Abraham to give the land to his seed.…God's fourth appearing to Abraham was in Genesis 13:14-17, when He told Abraham to lift up his eyes and look in every direction at the land.…The appearing of God in Genesis 15:1-7 was the fifth; it was nothing new to Abraham. God had appeared to Abraham repeatedly, and Abraham had experienced the riches of God's appearing, coming to have confidence in them. During the first four appearings, God's element had been transfused and infused into Abraham's being. When God appeared to Abraham, He did not leave suddenly. He stayed with Abraham for a length of time.…[In Genesis 18] He stayed with him for about half a day, conversing with him for hours as with an intimate friend. Throughout that whole visitation Abraham was infused with God. During the fifth appearing (Gen. 15) God told Abraham that the number of his seed would be like the stars of heaven. As a result of the fifth appearing, Abraham had experienced such a rich infusion of God that he believed. "And Abraham believed God, and it was accounted to him as righteousness" (Rom. 4:3; Gen. 15:6). (*Life-study of Romans,* pp. 78, 93-94)

Further Reading: Life-study of Romans, msg. 8

Enlightenment and inspiration: _____

_____
_____
_____

Morning Nourishment

Gal.
3:8 And the Scripture, foreseeing that God would justify the Gentiles out of faith, announced the gospel beforehand to Abraham: "In you shall all the nations be blessed."
14 In order that the blessing of Abraham might come to the Gentiles in Christ Jesus, that we might receive the promise of the Spirit through faith.

God is also seen as the God of blessing in His second calling with His second speaking to Abraham (Gen. 12:1-4). God not only called him but also promised to make of him a great country and make his name great....God not only blessed him but also made him a blessing to others. This blessing is the blessing of the New Testament gospel (Gal. 3:9, 14). (*The History of God in His Union with Man,* pp. 93-94)

Today's Reading

Abraham was a descendant of Shem, and we have seen that according to Noah's prophecy, God would be the God of Shem, and Japheth would dwell in the tents of Shem. Japheth received the blessing of being enlarged (Gen. 9:26-27). According to history, the Europeans as the sons of Japheth have expanded and spread all over the earth. The whole world has become the dwelling place of the Europeans....After Columbus discovered the Western world and through the development of transportation, the Europeans have spread everywhere. But they have to dwell in Shem's tent, which becomes a blessing to them. God made Abraham, a descendant of Shem, a blessing to others. This blessing is in the tent of Shem. Many people throughout the whole earth are enjoying the blessings of God in Shem's tent.

Every person needs a tent in which he can rest and enjoy life. God's blessing to Abraham which made him a blessing to others implies the tent of Shem. When the Lord Jesus came as a seed of Abraham and a descendant of Shem, He became the tent, the tabernacle (John 1:14), which will consummate in the New Jerusalem (Rev. 21:2-3). The New Jerusalem will be God's eternal tabernacle, His eternal tent, in which numerous Old Testament saints and New Testament believers from all the nations will dwell to participate in the eternal blessing of the eternal life. This is all implied in the blessing God gave to Abraham. (*The History of God in His Union with Man,* p. 94)

Galatians 3:14 indicates that the Spirit is the blessing that God promised to Abraham for all the nations and that has been received by the believers through faith in Christ. The Spirit is the compound Spirit...and actually is God Himself processed in His Trinity through incarnation, crucifixion, resurrection, ascension, and descension that we may receive Him as our life and our everything. This is the focus of the gospel of God.

The physical aspect of the blessing that God promised to Abraham was the good land (Gen. 12:7; 13:15; 17:8; 26:3-4), which was a type of the all-inclusive Christ (see Col. 1:12 and footnote 2). Since Christ is eventually realized as the all-inclusive life-giving Spirit (1 Cor. 15:45; 2 Cor. 3:17), the blessing of the promised Spirit corresponds with the blessing of the land promised to Abraham. Actually, the Spirit as the realization of Christ in our experience is the good land as the source of God's bountiful supply for us to enjoy. (Gal. 3:14, footnote 3)

The Spirit we have received of God is the total blessing of the gospel....In the gospel we have received not only the blessing of forgiveness, washing, and cleansing; we have received the blessing of the Triune God as the processed, all-inclusive, life-giving Spirit. This living, all-inclusive person is the blessing. Day by day, God is supplying this blessing to us, and we are receiving this blessing of God. Oh, how blessed we are! What a marvelous blessing we are enjoying! This unique blessing is the all-inclusive person of the Triune God—the Father, the Son, and the Spirit—processed to become the life-giving Spirit dwelling in us in a most subjective way for our enjoyment. (*Life-study of Galatians,* p. 300)

Further Reading: Life-study of Galatians, msg. 34

Enlightenment and inspiration: _____

_____

_____

_____

Morning Nourishment

Gen. And Jehovah appeared to Abram and said, To your
12:7 seed I will give this land...
13:14-15 And Jehovah said to Abram after Lot had separated from him, Now lift up your eyes, and look from
the place where you are, northward and southward
and eastward and westward; for all the land that
you see I will give to you and to your seed forever.

God is revealed as the God of the earth, in His second appearing with His third speaking, in promising Abraham that He
would give the land of Canaan to his seed (Gen. 12:6-7). In His
first appearing, God called Abraham. In His second appearing,
He promised Abraham that He would give the land of Canaan to
his seed. Abraham's seed, generally speaking, refers to his earthly
descendants, the Jews, Israel. But narrowly speaking, the seed
refers to Christ (Gal. 3:16).

The Jews...will not fully inherit [the land] until the time of res-
toration when Christ returns. Christ will return as the unique seed
of Abraham and will inherit the good land from the Great Sea, the
Mediterranean, to the Great River, the Euphrates. There have
been disputes and conferences about the boundaries of the nation
of Israel for years, but when Jesus comes back as the unique seed
of Abraham, He will clear up the situation and inherit the good
land. (*The History of God in His Union with Man,* pp. 94-95)

Today's Reading

God gave this land to Abraham's seed because God is the God
of the land, the God, the Owner, of the earth. The earthly governments may think that their respective territories belong to
them, but actually the entire earth belongs to Jehovah God (Psa.
24:1)....As the Possessor and Owner of the land, He has the
right to give it to His friend's descendants.

The God of Abraham is seen as the God of secret care for His
elect in saving [His friend] Abraham from Pharaoh's insulting of
his wife (Gen. 12:10-20)....He is the God of secret care for His
elect to rescue His elect from their troubles.

God is seen as the God of comfort and encouragement in His fourth speaking to Abraham after Lot left him....God promised to give to Abraham and to his seed the land of Canaan as far as he could see in four directions and to make his seed as numerous as the dust of the earth (Gen. 13:14-17). Abraham and Lot both became rich. They had many flocks, herds, and tents, and the land was too small for them to dwell together. Then Abraham asked Lot to choose the part of the land that he desired, and Lot left him.

Abraham was left in a lonely state. His father was dead, and his nephew Lot departed. Then God came to comfort and encourage him in promising to give him and his seed the land of Canaan as far as he could see and to make his seed as numerous as the dust of the earth. No one can count how many descendants God has given to Abraham, because they are innumerable. Many of his descendants were killed by the four kinds of locusts in Joel 1:4, signifying the Gentile governments with their invading armies. These locusts were like the waves from the Mediterranean Sea, which came to scour Israel as the dust. But regardless of how much the water washed away the dust, there was still some sand left. This is why in Genesis 22:17, Abraham's descendants are not likened to the dust but to the sand on the seashore. Some of Abraham's descendants are in the heavens as the stars.

The God of Abraham is seen as the God Most High, the Possessor of heaven and earth, in His divine supply with His blessing to Abraham through His priest Melchizedek after Abraham fought the battle against the four kings (Gen. 14:17-20). He is not only the God of the heaven but also the God of the earth, so He is the Most High....In that victory he recovered Lot and his family with their possessions (v. 16)....The priest of God came to serve him with bread and wine as a kind of refreshment, and that refreshment resembled the Lord's table (Matt. 26:26-28). In the Lord's table, He supplies us and refreshes us, the tired, weary sinners. (*The History of God in His Union with Man,* pp. 95-96)

Further Reading: The History of God in His Union with Man, ch. 7

Enlightenment and inspiration: _____

_____

_____

_____

Morning Nourishment

Gen. **And He brought him outside and said, Look now**
15:5-6 **toward the heavens, and count the stars, if you are**
able to count them. And He said to him, So shall
your seed be. And he believed Jehovah, and He
accounted it to him as righteousness.

The God of Abraham is revealed as the God of shield and great
reward in His fifth speaking (this time in a vision) to Abraham
(Gen. 15:1-6). A vision is a kind of divine scenery, not a physical
scenery....After defeating the four kings, Abraham may have
been afraid of their avenging. Thus, God came in to tell Abraham
that He would be a shield to protect him. He would also be Abraham's reward for his rescue of Lot. God was concerned for Lot, and
Abraham cooperated with God to rescue him. This was a real
credit to Abraham before God, so God rewarded him for this. This
shows us that God is very fine in taking care of His people.

God also promised Abraham that his heavenly seed in their
divine nature would be as many as the stars in heaven who
could never be touched by anyone on earth. Abraham believed in
Jehovah, and Jehovah reckoned this believing to him for righteousness (vv. 5-6). In Romans 4 Paul considered this as the
example of justification. God is the shield, God is the great
reward, and God is also the Justifier. God's justifying of Abraham meant that God became happy with Abraham and that
Abraham was altogether in harmony with God. He was altogether acceptable to God, having no problem with God. (*The His-*
tory of God in His Union with Man, pp. 96-97)

Today's Reading

In Genesis 15:1-6 God spoke to Abraham in a vision. In
15:12-21 God went on to speak to him when he was in a deep
sleep. God spoke to Abraham in a dream, foretelling that his
earthly seed in their human nature as "the dust of the earth"
(13:16) would be sojourners in Egypt. They would be aliens in a
foreign country and live there, serve the Egyptians, be afflicted
by them for four hundred years, and in the fourth generation

return to Canaan. Because of His faithfulness in keeping His promise, He also made a covenant with him to assure him of His faithfulness in His promise that He has given to his seed the land from the river of Egypt, the Nile, to the Great River, Euphrates. Such a covenant was a confirmation of God's promise to Abraham in 12:7 and 13:14-17.

God is also seen as the God of silence to Abraham. This was due to the fact that Abraham listened to his wife Sarah and married Hagar to get a son by the exercise of his flesh when he was eighty-six years old (Gen. 16:1-4, 15-16). That offended God to the uttermost.

In spite of God's repeated promise and His confirming covenant [Gen. 12—15], in Genesis 16 Abraham's wife proposed that he take Hagar her maid to bear a child for her (vv. 1-3). Abraham took, by exercising his flesh, Hagar and she bore a son by the name of Ishmael. This was a real offense to God! And God became silent to Abraham for that long time of thirteen years.

When Abraham was ninety-nine years old, God came in to reconfirm His covenant, which became a covenant of circumcision (Gen. 17:9-14). In God's third appearing with His seventh speaking to Abraham, He is the God of all-sufficiency in being the God of circumcision to cut off His chosen people's natural man in the flesh that they may become God's new creation, signified by Isaac who was born by God's grace, not as Ishmael who was born by Abraham's flesh (Gen. 17:1-21; Gal. 4:22-31).

Circumcision is the cutting off of the flesh, signifying that the flesh of our fallen man, our natural man, has to be cut off, ended, terminated. The apostle Paul said that the physical circumcision in the Old Testament was a full type of the crucifixion of Christ in dealing with the flesh of our body (Col. 2:11). Christ's death on the cross, His crucifixion, is our real circumcision which cuts off our flesh with its passions and its lusts (Gal. 5:24). (*The History of God in His Union with Man,* pp. 97-99)

Further Reading: The History of God in His Union with Man, ch. 7

Enlightenment and inspiration: _____

_____

_____
_____

Morning Nourishment

Gen. And when Abram was ninety-nine years old, Jeho-
17:1-2 vah appeared to Abram and said to him, I am the
        All-sufficient God; walk before Me, and be per-
        fect. And I will make My covenant between Me and
        you, and I will multiply you exceedingly.
   10   This is My covenant, which you shall keep, be-
        tween Me and you and your seed after you: Every
        male among you shall be circumcised.

Circumcision indicates that God wants our natural man to be
cut off. Then God wants us to be reborn by His grace in resurrection, typified by Isaac. Thus, Genesis 17 reveals Christ's crucifixion and resurrection. The crucifixion is to cut off the old man; the
resurrection is to bring forth, or to beget, the new man, and the
new man is signified by Isaac. (*The History of God in His Union
with Man,* p. 99)

Today's Reading

God would recognize only the people brought forth by Christ's
resurrection as the legal seed of Abraham (Gal. 3:29)....First
Peter 1:3 says that we all have been regenerated by the resurrection of Christ. Christ's crucifixion is a termination, and His resurrection is a germination. Christ's death terminated our old
man, and Christ's resurrection germinated our new man to
make us the new creation.

Isaac was born of the free woman, born of grace. He was a
pattern of the New Testament believers. We, the New Testament believers, are all born of the free woman, the grace of God.
Thus, Isaac as Abraham's seed typifies both Christ (Gal. 3:16)
and all of the New Testament believers (v. 29). Christ is the
Head and the believers are His Body. Isaac was not born by the
flesh of the old man but by God's grace in resurrection.

In Genesis 17:1 God appeared to Abraham and declared to
him that He is the God of all-sufficiency. Most of the versions
translate this as "the Almighty God," but the Hebrew word here
indicates all-sufficiency. Genesis 17 actually covers the new

covenant, the new testament. God's economy in the New Testament is all-sufficient. In the New Testament we have everything. We have the death of Christ to cut off our old man, and we have the new birth through Christ's resurrection. Through Christ's death and resurrection, we have everything in the New Testament. Philippians 1:19 indicates that the Spirit of Jesus Christ has a bountiful supply that is all-sufficient.

God with His human friendship came (in His fourth appearing with His eighth speaking to Abraham) as a man, in the form of a man, to visit Abraham as His friend (2 Chron. 20:7; Isa. 41:8; James 2:23) on the level of humanity (Gen. 18—19).

The first time God visited man was when He visited Adam. Adam became fallen and God came to seek him. God asked Adam, "Where are you?" (Gen. 3:9). With Abraham, God's visit was different. He came to visit Abraham as His friend on the level of humanity, not on the level of divinity. God did not appear to Abraham as a divine being but as a human being. As a man God came to talk to Abraham, and Abraham gave Him water for Him to wash His feet. Abraham also served this One a meal prepared by his wife. This is all on the human level.

Abraham walked with God, and God conversed with Abraham as one human friend to another....Abraham walked with God as with a man, and God conversed with Abraham as a human friend. He spoke to Abraham concerning His judgment of Sodom, where Abraham's nephew Lot and his family lived. God came to His friend to rescue His friend's nephew. Again, we can see God's hidden care, His secret care, for Lot as one of His elect.

The God with friendship in humanity is revealed in His sending of Abraham's nephew and his two daughters out from the overthrow of Sodom, for the remembrance of Abraham as His intimate friend (Gen. 19:29, 12-22). The God of Abraham is a God of human friendship, and Abraham's God is our God. (*The History of God in His Union with Man*, pp. 99-101)

Further Reading: Life-study of Romans, msg. 7

Enlightenment and inspiration: _____

_____

_____
_____

Morning Nourishment

Gen.   Now after these things God tested Abraham and
22:1-2 said to him, Abraham. And he said, Here I am. And
He said, Take now your son, your only son, whom
you love, Isaac, and go to the land of Moriah, and
offer him there as a burnt offering on one of the
mountains of which I will tell you.

8 And Abraham said, God Himself will provide the
lamb for a burnt offering, my son...

Abraham's offering of his beloved and only son, Isaac, on the altar is a vivid picture of God the Father's offering of His beloved and only Son, Jesus Christ, on the cross. In this picture Isaac typifies Christ in a detailed way. Isaac, as Abraham's only son (Gen. 22:2, 12, 16), typifies Christ as God's only begotten Son (John 3:16). Isaac was Abraham's beloved son (Gen. 22:2), and Christ was the Father's beloved Son, in whom He delighted (Matt. 3:17). Isaac took his father's will (Gen. 22:6), and Christ also chose the will of His Father (Matt. 26:39). Isaac was obedient unto death (Gen. 22:9-10); likewise, Christ was obedient unto death (Phil. 2:8). Isaac carried the wood for the burnt offering and walked to the top of Mount Moriah (Gen. 22:6); in the same way, Christ bore His cross and walked to Golgotha (John 19:17)....Isaac was "killed" on the altar and was returned to Abraham on the third day, that is, in resurrection (Gen. 22:4, 10-13; Heb. 11:19); similarly, Christ was crucified on the cross and was resurrected on the third day (1 Cor. 15:4). Isaac was multiplied in resurrection (Gen. 22:17), and Christ also was multiplied in His resurrection (John 12:24; 1 Pet. 1:3). Isaac was the seed of Abraham for the blessing of all the nations (Gen. 22:18); likewise, Christ is the unique seed of Abraham in whom the blessing of Abraham has come to the nations (Gal. 3:8, 14, 16). (Gen. 22:2, footnote 1)

Today's Reading

Genesis 20 shows us the almighty God with His friendly care, in saving His close friend Abraham, with His almighty power, from the loss of his wife to Abimelech, king of Gerar. God caused that king's family to lose the capacity to beget children (vv. 17-18). That was God's exercise of His almighty power. Then God told that king that Abraham would pray for him. Abraham later prayed for him, and the women of his house were healed. God exercised a friendly care for Abraham by His almighty power.

God is also the God of changelessness in keeping the principle of His grace, in recognizing Isaac, Abraham's son of Sarah, as his only son, in His ninth speaking to Abraham (Gen. 21:1-12). The God of Abraham is the God of changelessness in keeping His word, His promise.

Genesis 22:11-14 reveals the Triune God of provision, in His providing a ram to replace Isaac for a burnt offering to God (as the Angel of Jehovah—Christ). This was God's eleventh speaking to Abraham. The One who spoke to Abraham was Jehovah, yet this was the Angel of Jehovah. Therefore, in Genesis 22 we see Christ in two aspects. Christ is typified as a ram and is seen as the Angel of Jehovah. The ram is the substitute for sinners, and the Angel of Jehovah is the One who serves Jehovah in taking care of God's friend.

The Triune God of blessing, in His twelfth (last) speaking to Abraham, promised him that He (as the Angel of Jehovah—Christ) would bless him and multiply his seed as the stars of the heaven and as the sand upon the seashore, and in Abraham's seed (Christ) all the nations of the earth would be blessed (Gen. 22:15-18).

The God of Abraham is seen as the God of friendship on the human level, in leading the old servant of His friend Abraham to secure a wife for his son Isaac (Gen. 24). Though this was not directly motivated by God, it was carried out by God. Abraham charged his old servant to find Isaac a wife, and his old servant did it by following God's leading. (*The History of God in His Union with Man,* pp. 101-103)

Further Reading: The History of God in His Union with Man, ch. 7

Enlightenment and inspiration: _____

_____

_____

_____

Hymns, #1190

1   O Lord, You've called to us, and Canaan we would win,
To be Your corporate man and dwell with You therein;
But how the darkness of this world does hold us in —
   O Lord, appear to us, we pray.

      O Lord, appear to us today;
      We see this is the only way.
      The idols to forsake
      And Canaan land partake,
      O Lord, appear to us today.

2   O God of glory, shine; draw and we'll follow You.
Our strength and motive be, it's nothing we could do.
Your light attracts us, Lord, 'til all else fades from
   view —
   O Lord, do shine on us, we pray.

      O Lord, do shine on us today;
      Till all our background fades away,
      Till You alone we see,
      Shining so gloriously —
      O Lord, do shine on us today.

3   In Your appearing, Lord, we have Your speaking clear;
Your word empowers us and drives away all fear.
So, Lord, keep calling us, Your voice we need to hear.
   O Lord, do speak to us, we pray.

      O Lord, do speak in us today;
      You know the words You need to say.
      To open all our heart,
      Your very Self impart.
      O Lord, do speak in us today.

4   O Lord, it's not of us, we've seen it's all of You;
You are the calling One, Originator too!
We can receive this call by our beholding You —
   O God of glory, come, we pray.

O God of glory, come today;
We've seen this is the only way
To answer Your dear call
That You might be our all —
O God of glory, come today.

Composition for prophecy with main point and sub-points: _____

_____
_____
_____
_____
_____
_____
_____
_____
_____
_____
_____
_____
_____
_____
_____
_____
_____
_____
_____
_____
_____
_____
_____
_____
_____
_____
_____
_____
_____
_____
_____
_____
_____
_____
_____
_____
_____

Living a Grace-enjoying Life
for God's Good Pleasure

Scripture Reading: Gen. 26:3-4, 12-33; Gal. 6:18; 1 Cor. 15:10; 2 Cor. 12:7-10; Rev. 22:21

Day 1

I. **Isaac is a model, a pattern, of the enjoyment of God's grace for God's good pleasure (Gen. 24:36; 25:5; 26:3-4, 12-33; Rom. 5:1-2; Acts 4:33; 11:23):**
  A. Grace is God in Christ as the Spirit wrought into our being for our enjoyment to be everything to us and to do everything in us, through us, and for us so that He can become the constituent of our being for the building up of the Body of Christ to consummate the New Jerusalem (John 1:16-17; Heb. 10:29b; 1 Cor. 15:10; cf. Gal. 2:20; 2 Cor. 13:14).
  B. It is our destiny to enjoy the grace of God; this destiny was preordained before the foundation of the world (Eph. 1:3-6; 2:7).

Day 2

  C. *El Shaddai,* the All-sufficient God, is the all-sufficient grace to supply His called ones with the riches of His divine being that they might bring forth Christ as the seed for the fulfillment of His purpose (Gen. 17:1; 28:3; 2 Cor. 12:9; Phil. 1:19-21a).

II. **After Abraham's natural strength and self-effort were dealt with by God, Isaac was born (Gen. 17:15-19; 18:10-14; 21:1-7); this implies that Isaac was born of grace, which is represented by Sarah (Gal. 4:23-28, 31; 1 Pet. 3:7):**
  A. "Is anything too marvelous for Jehovah? At the appointed time I will return to you, according to the time of life, and Sarah shall have a son" (Gen. 18:14):
    1. The time of life (v. 10), the appointed time for the birth of Isaac (17:21), was the time of God's visitation (21:1).

2. The birth of Isaac was the coming of Jehovah, which was the coming of grace (cf. John 1:17).

3. Isaac was born by the strength of God's grace, not by the strength of man's natural life; this took place after Abraham had been circumcised and he and his wife, Sarah, had been completely deadened (Gen. 18:11; Rom. 4:18-19), signifying that the time of life, the time when Christ will be life to us, will come after our natural strength has been terminated.

B. Abraham's life reveals that if we would enjoy God's grace and have the full enjoyment of His riches, we must suffer loss and have our natural life circumcised, cut off; the greatest frustration to knowing and experiencing grace is the self (Gen. 17:11, 19; cf. Phil. 3:3).

C. Isaac's life reveals that our suffering to terminate our natural life is for the enjoyment of God's grace (cf. 2 Cor. 1:8-9, 12; 12:7-10; Rom. 5:1-5).

Day 3 **III. Isaac was grown up in grace; to grow in grace is to grow in the enjoyment of all that Christ is to us as our spiritual food and living water (Gen. 21:8; 2 Pet. 3:18; 1 Pet. 2:2; 1 Cor. 3:2, 6; Eph. 3:8; 4:15):**

A. The growth of Isaac signifies the growth of Christ in the New Testament believers after He is born in them; the growth of Christ in us is needed so that Christ can be formed in us (1 Cor. 3:6; Gal. 4:19; *Hymns,* #395).

B. The Spirit of grace (Heb. 10:29) is the grace of life (1 Pet. 3:7), the varied grace of God (4:10), the God of all grace (5:10), and the all-sufficient grace (2 Cor. 12:9); this grace is now with our spirit (Gal. 6:18).

C. The way to daily receive and enjoy grace is through the blood, the word, the Spirit, and the church:

1. The redeeming blood, the blood of the covenant, God's own blood, brings sinful, corrupted people into the eternal enjoyment of God (Acts 20:28; Matt. 26:28; Lev. 16:11-16; Heb. 10:19-20; 1 John 1:7, 9).
2. The word of grace can be eaten by us and become to us the gladness and joy of our heart (Acts 20:32; Jer. 15:16; John 6:63).
3. The Spirit of grace as the bountiful supply of the processed and consummated God is the oil of exultant joy with which we are anointed as the partners of Christ (Heb. 1:9; 10:29b; Zech. 12:10a).
4. The church of God experiences the fresh and refreshing grace of God as the descending dew, which comes to us from the heavens through God's compassions to water and transform us (Psa. 133:3; Lam. 3:22-23; 2 Cor. 13:14; Acts 11:23).

Day 4 D. The way to daily receive and enjoy grace is to turn to the spirit, exercise the spirit, and enthrone the Lord (Heb. 4:16; Rom. 5:17, 21; cf. Rev. 4:2):

1. God's throne is the source of the flowing grace; whenever we fail to enthrone the Lord, dethroning Him, the flow of grace stops (22:1; Col. 1:18b; Rev. 2:4; 1 Pet. 5:5).
2. If we enthrone the Lord Jesus within us, the Spirit as the river of water of life will flow out from the throne of grace to supply us; in this way we shall receive grace and enjoy grace (Rev. 22:1; *Hymns,* #770).

E. The way to daily receive and enjoy grace is to love the Lord, consecrate ourselves to the Lord, and contact the Lord in His Word by means of all prayer (2 Cor. 5:14; Eph. 6:24; Lev. 6:12-13; Eph. 6:17-18; Acts 20:32).

IV. **Isaac also became the heir in grace; we too are heirs of God, enjoying Him as the pledge**

of our inheritance for us to inherit Him and
for Him to inherit us (Gen. 21:9-12; 24:36; 25:5;
Rom. 8:17; Acts 26:18; Eph. 1:11, 14, 18):

Day 5   A. Isaac inherited all things from his father (Gen.
          24:36; 25:5); in the New Testament all the called
          believers are heirs of God's absolute and uncon-
          ditional grace, inheriting all the riches of the
          divine fullness for our enjoyment (Eph. 1:3, 6;
          3:8, 19).

       B. Isaac signifies that we do not do anything our-
          selves or seek for anything ourselves; Isaac is
          the enjoyment of everything of Abraham, signify-
          ing everything of the Father (Gen. 24:36; 25:5).

       C. Knowing the God of Isaac means only one
          thing: knowing God as the Supplier and that ev-
          erything comes from Him; it also means that
          everything comes by receiving and that receiving
          is the secret to victory (Eph. 1:3; Phil. 1:19; John
          1:16; Rom. 5:17; 8:2).

 V. Isaac obeyed in grace; whenever we obey in
    grace, we shall meet the provision of God
    (Gen. 22:5-10; John 1:17):

       A. God's grace is powerful, enabling us to bear any-
          thing (2 Tim. 2:1).

       B. Grace can reign over all things (Rom. 5:21; Heb.
          4:16).

       C. To go back to the law is to reject this grace, to
          nullify this grace, to fall from grace (Gal. 2:21;
          5:4; cf. Gen. 16:16; 17:1):

          1. To fall from grace is to be brought to nought,
             reduced to nothing, separated from Christ,
             deprived of all profit from Christ (cf. John
             15:4-5).

          2. If we go to anything other than Christ, such
             as the law or character improvement, and
             do not cleave to Christ so that we may enjoy
             Him all the time, our enjoyment of Christ
             will be confiscated (cf. Col. 2:18).

       D. We need to be confirmed by grace, which is to

remain in the new covenant to enjoy Christ as
grace (Heb. 13:9; Gal. 5:4).

VI. **Isaac received a hundredfold harvest, "and
the man became rich and continued to grow
richer until he became very rich"; our hearts
need to be the good earth where Christ can
bear fruit a hundredfold, and we need to be
rich toward God, enjoying grace upon grace
(Gen. 26:12-14; Luke 8:8, 15; 12:15-21; Eph. 3:8;
John 1:16).**

Day 6 VII. **Although Isaac enjoyed God's unconditional
grace, finding enjoyment and satisfaction (signified by a well) in every place that he went
(Gen. 25:11; 26:15-25, 33), Beer-sheba was the
unique place in which he experienced God's
appearing, received His promise, built an
altar, called on the name of the Lord, and
pitched a tent as a testimony:**

A. God's called ones are destined to enjoy God's
grace regardless of their standing, but this enjoyment does not justify their standing.

B. If we desire to have God's appearing, inherit His
promises, and live a life for the fulfillment of His
eternal purpose, we must come to the unique
place that God has chosen and remain there.

C. This unique place is signified by Beer-sheba,
with the well for life supply and the tamarisk
tree as the expression of the rich flow of life
(vv. 23-24; 21:25, 33).

VIII. **Isaac inherited the promise that God had
given to his father concerning the good land
and the unique seed, which is Christ, in whom
all the nations of the earth will be blessed
(26:3-5; Gal. 3:14, 16):**

A. The unique seed of Abraham as the last Adam
became the life-giving Spirit, who is the blessing
of Abraham (the reality of the good land), for the
dispensing of Himself into the believers of Christ
to make them the corporate seed of Abraham

(vv. 14, 16, 29; 1 Cor. 15:45b; John 12:24; Isa. 53:10).

B. This promise was for the fulfillment of God's purpose so that God might have a kingdom on the earth in which to express Himself through a corporate people (Gen. 1:26; Mark 4:26; Dan. 2:34-35).

C. Through our enjoyment of grace, the kingdom of God will be realized, and God in Christ will be fully expressed for eternity (Rev. 22:21; Eph. 2:10).

Morning Nourishment

Gen. And Abraham gave all that he had to Isaac.
25:5
26:12 And Isaac sowed in that land and gained in the same
        year a hundredfold. And Jehovah blessed him.
Acts And with great power the apostles gave testimony
4:33 of the resurrection of the Lord Jesus, and great
        grace was upon them all.

Isaac was a model, a pattern, of the enjoyment of God's grace. In the whole Bible there is hardly another person who enjoyed grace as much as Isaac did. Throughout his entire life Isaac did nothing except enjoy the grace of God. His life was a grace-enjoying life. Nevertheless, in Isaac we see exactly the same natural weakness as we saw in Abraham. Furthermore, in Isaac we also see the natural life of Jacob....According to our natural concept, a person who has a natural weakness and who lives in the natural life can never enjoy the grace of God. This is our concept; it is not God's word. In the Bible, we cannot see that Isaac was very spiritual. He was a man who still had a natural weakness and who still lived in the natural life. Why then did he have such an enjoyment of God's grace? Simply because God had ordained it that way. With us Christians, there is the aspect of God's ordination. (*Life-study of Genesis,* pp. 847-848)

Today's Reading

It is our destiny to enjoy the grace of God. This destiny was preordained before the foundation of the world. Do not think that if you are spiritual, you are privileged to enjoy God's grace and that if you are not spiritual, you cannot enjoy His grace. This is a religious concept, and the Bible does not teach this. After hearing that enjoying grace does not depend upon our being spiritual, some may say, "If we don't need to be spiritual to enjoy God's grace, then let us be unspiritual." Do not say this. Neither being spiritual nor being unspiritual will help us to enjoy God's grace. It is entirely a matter of God's ordination, and it does not depend on what we are nor on what we can do. With us, there is the aspect of

Isaac. We have been ordained by God to the enjoyment of grace.... Do not waste your time trying to be spiritual or trying to be unspiritual. Simply say, "O Lord, I worship You for Your ordination. You have ordained me to the enjoyment of grace." At the least, we all are a part of Isaac. In our being there is the aspect of having been ordained by God to the enjoyment of His grace.

The matter of grace has been hidden, concealed, and veiled throughout the years. What is grace? Grace is something of God which is wrought into our being and which works in us and does things for us. It is nothing outward. Grace is God in Christ wrought into our being to live, work, and do things for us. In 1 Corinthians 15:10 Paul says, "By the grace of God I am what I am; and His grace unto me was not in vain, but I labored more abundantly than all of them, yet not I, but the grace of God with me." This word is quite deep. Paul did not say, "By the grace of God I have what I have. I have a good car, a good job, and a good wife by the grace of God." He did not even say, "By the grace of God I do what I do." It is not a matter of doing, having, or working; it is absolutely a matter of being. Hence, Paul says, "By the grace of God I am what I am." This means that the very grace of God had been wrought into his being, making him that kind of person. In Galatians 2:20 Paul says, "No longer I who live, but it is Christ who lives in me." If we put this verse together with 1 Corinthians 15:10, we see that grace is simply Christ living in us. It is "not I, but the grace of God," "no longer I...but...Christ." Grace is not outside of us or beside us. It is a divine person, God Himself in Christ, wrought into our being to be the constituent of our being. Because of the lack of revelation, Christians have misunderstood and misinterpreted grace, thinking of it as something outside of them. But grace is just the Triune God wrought into our being to be what we should be and to live, work, and do things for us so that we may say, "I am what I am by the grace of God. It is not I, but the grace of God." (*Life-study of Genesis,* pp. 848-849, 828-829)

Further Reading: Life-study of Genesis, msg. 65

Enlightenment and inspiration: _____

_____

_____

_____

Morning Nourishment

Gen. **And when Abram was ninety-nine years old, Jeho-**
17:1 **vah appeared to Abram and said to him, I am the**
All-sufficient God; walk before Me, and be perfect.
18:14 **Is anything too marvelous for Jehovah? At the**
appointed time I will return to you, according to
the time of life, and Sarah shall have a son.

[In Genesis 17:1 the Hebrew word for All-sufficient God is] *El Shaddai. El* means *the Mighty One,* and *Shaddai* comes from the Hebrew word meaning *breast* or *udder.* This divine title reveals God as the Mighty One with an udder, that is, the all-sufficient Mighty One. He is the source of grace to supply His called ones with the riches of His divine being that they may bring forth Christ as the seed for the fulfillment of His purpose. (Gen. 17:1, footnote 2)

After Abraham's natural strength and self-effort were dealt with by God, Isaac was born (Gen. 17:15-19; 18:10-14; 21:1-7). This implies that Isaac was born of grace, which is represented by Sarah (Gal. 4:24-28, 31). The record of Genesis says this transpired at "the time of life" (Gen. 18:10, 14). Whenever the effort of the natural life ceases, that is the time of life....Something is born in grace. Grace is related to life, and life goes with grace. Hence, grace is called "the grace of life" (1 Pet. 3:7). (*Life-study of Genesis,* p. 832)

Today's Reading

The birth of Isaac was the coming of Jehovah, which was the coming of grace (cf. John 1:17). Isaac was born by the strength of God's grace, not by the strength of man's natural life. This took place after Abraham had been circumcised and he and his wife, Sarah, had become completely deadened (Gen. 18:11; Rom. 4:18-19), signifying that the time of life, the time when Christ will be life to us, will come after our natural strength has been terminated. (Gen. 18:14, footnote 1)

God wants to bring us into the enjoyment of grace, but there is a frustration to this grace—the self. We ourselves are the frustration. Although Christ has come and grace has come with Him, and although we have been brought into the grace in which we stand, the greatest frustration to this grace is you and I. Hence, before we can have the experience of Isaac, we need Abraham who represents the first aspect of the experience of life. Abraham's life reveals that if we would enjoy God's grace and have the full enjoyment of God's riches, we must be dealt with, circumcised, and cut off....Isaac came after Abraham's circumcision. After Abraham was circumcised in Genesis 17, God told him that Isaac would be born (17:19)....God's visitation equals the birth of Isaac. God visited Sarah and that visitation became the birth of Isaac. This is grace.

God has come to be enjoyed by His called ones. But if we would have this enjoyment, the self must go. Once the self has gone, Isaac comes. This means that grace comes. It is not easy to lose the self. In order for the self to go, we must suffer loss....After Abraham was circumcised, Isaac came. This is the principle. With us, the self must go and then grace will come. We must firstly be Abraham and then we become Isaac.

If we love others in ourselves, God will never recognize that love, because it does not come from His visitation. God wants to visit us, get into us, live for us, and even love others for us. He will only recognize that kind of love. Your love is an Ishmael; the love by God's visitation is an Isaac. Whether you are humble or proud, crooked or straight, means nothing. God does not recognize anything which comes out of you apart from His visitation. Whatever is not of grace is not recognized, not counted, by God. We all must say, "O Lord, I will not do anything without Your visitation. Lord, if You will not visit me and work something through me and out of me, I will do nothing. I will neither hate nor love, be proud nor be humble. I want to be blank. Lord, without Your visitation, I am nothing." God's visitation is the practical grace. When I love others and am humble by God's visitation, not by my self-effort, that is the enjoyment of grace. (*Life-study of Genesis,* pp. 825-826, 829)

Further Reading: Life-study of Genesis, msg. 63

Enlightenment and inspiration: _____

_____

_____

_____

Morning Nourishment

Gen. **And the child grew and was weaned. And Abra-**
21:8 **ham made a great feast on the day that Isaac was**
weaned.
Gal. **The grace of our Lord Jesus Christ be with your**
6:18 **spirit, brothers. Amen.**
1 Pet. **As newborn babes, long for the guileless milk of**
2:2 **the word in order that by it you may grow unto sal-**
vation.

Isaac was grown up in grace (Gen. 21:8). By his history we see that he did not do anything. He was born and he was grown up. I do not say that he grew up, but that he was grown up. Like a farmer who grows apples in his orchard, God grew Isaac like a tree in His orchard. Isaac was grown up by God in grace.

Second Peter 3:18 tells us to "grow in the grace." This indicates that to grow is the feeding and watering as revealed by Peter in 1 Peter 2:2 and by Paul in 1 Corinthians 3:2 and 6. To grow in grace is to grow in the enjoyment of all that Christ is to us as our spiritual food and living water. All the riches of what Christ is to us are for our growth in life. The more we enjoy the riches of Christ (Eph. 3:8), the more we grow in life (Eph. 4:15). (*Life-study of Genesis,* p. 832)

Today's Reading

Grace is God working Himself into our being as our enjoyment. The very God today is not only God the Father, but also God the Son and God the Spirit. Moreover, God the Spirit is the Spirit of grace (Heb. 10:29), and this grace is the grace of life (1 Pet. 3:7), which is "the varied grace" (1 Pet. 4:10), the "all grace" (1 Pet. 5:10), and the sufficient grace (2 Cor. 12:9). The Triune God is such a grace, and this grace is now with our spirit (Gal. 6:18). Grace is the divine Person of the Triune God as the Spirit indwelling our spirit. It is by the Spirit of grace indwelling our spirit to be our enjoyment that we may enjoy God as our life and our everything, even as our living. This is why every one of Paul's Epistles ends with the words, "Grace be with you." For example, 2 Corinthians 13:14 says, "The grace of the Lord Jesus Christ and the love of God and the fellowship of the Holy Spirit be with you all." Grace is not outside of us; it is in us. Whatever we call it, the Spirit of grace or the grace of life, it is something living and divine in our spirit. We do have such a divine reality, the Triune God Himself, in our spirit as our grace and enjoyment. When He loves others through us, this love is our enjoyment. When He lives Himself out through us, this living is also our enjoyment. Day and night we may enjoy His living through us.

Why then do we suffer? Because the self, the ego, the natural man, is still here and must be dealt with. Praise Him that no dealing is in vain. Every dealing from God is a breaking of our natural man that we may enjoy more of Him as our grace. Thus, we have Abraham and Isaac; we have the suffering of the loss and the enjoyment of the gain. This gain is not the gain of outward things; it is the gain of the indwelling One, that is, the Spirit of grace and the grace of life. Again I say, whatever God gives as a gift outside of us is, at the most, a blessing. When this gift is wrought into our being, becoming the life element within us, it is grace. The blessing must become the grace. In the Old Testament, God gave many things to His people as blessings, but all those things were merely outward blessings. Before Christ came, none of those blessings had been wrought into God's people. Christ came not only to die on the cross for us, but, after His death, to become the life-giving Spirit to enter into our being. Thus, in the New Testament, we have the terms "in Christ" and "Christ in you." Now He is in us and we are in Him. Whatever God gives us in Christ has been wrought into our being and has become grace, our enjoyment. Now we are not merely under His blessing; we are in His grace and His grace is in us. What are you enjoying today—blessing or grace? The New Testament never says, "Blessing be with you." Rather, it says repeatedly, "Grace be with you." (*Life-study of Genesis,* pp. 831-832)

Further Reading: CWWN, vol. 35, "The God of Abraham, Isaac, and Jacob," ch. 7

Enlightenment and inspiration: _____

_____

_____

_____

Morning Nourishment

Heb. Let us therefore come forward with boldness to
4:16 the throne of grace that we may receive mercy and
find grace for timely help.
Rev. And he showed me a river of water of life, bright as
22:1 crystal, proceeding out of the throne of God and of
the Lamb in the middle of its street.

Our spirit is the only place we can experience grace. Just as electricity can be applied only by turning on the switch, so we can contact the moving, anointing Spirit only in our spirit. If you wish to receive grace and enjoy grace, do not exercise your mind, emotion, or will. Instead, turn to your spirit and exercise it.

There can be no doubt that, on the one hand, [the Lord] is on the throne in heaven. But, on the other hand, for our experience He is in our spirit. [In] Hebrews 4:16...the throne of grace is not only in heaven; it is also in our spirit....When I turn to my spirit and call, "Lord Jesus," I immediately have the sense that the throne of grace is in my spirit. (*Life-study of Galatians,* pp. 327-328)

Today's Reading

Whenever we approach the throne of grace by turning to our spirit and calling on the name of the Lord, we should enthrone the Lord. We must give Him the headship, kingship, and lordship in us....Whenever we fail to enthrone the Lord, the flow of grace stops. At the very time we are praying, we need to allow the Lord to be on the throne within us, honoring Him as the Head, the Lord, and the King. Then grace will flow within us as a river.

In Revelation 22:1 and 2 we see that the river of water of life proceeds out of the throne of God and of the Lamb. God's throne is thus the source of the flowing grace. To dethrone Him, to take the throne away from Him, is to disregard the source of grace. This causes the flow of grace to cease. This is not a mere doctrine but something very experiential. Many of us can testify that whenever we fail to enthrone the Lord, we do not receive much grace in our times of prayer.

The best way to practice turning to the spirit and staying in the spirit is to have fixed times for prayer. Suppose you set aside ten minutes in the morning to contact the Lord in prayer. During this time, the only thing you should do is exercise yourself to turn to the spirit and stay in the spirit. Do not be concerned about all the things you must do that day. Reject your natural mind, emotion, and will and exercise your spirit to contact the Lord.

When we turn to the spirit and stay there, we need to recognize the Lord as the Head and the King and enthrone Him. We need to respect His position, honor His authority, and confess that we have no right to say or do anything on our own. All the ground within us must be given over to the King. If we enthrone the Lord within us, the river of water of life will flow out from the throne to supply us. In this way we shall receive grace and enjoy grace.

Grace is nothing less than the Triune God becoming our enjoyment. The Father is embodied in the Son, and the Son is realized as the Spirit. This Spirit, the ultimate consummation of the Triune God, now dwells in our spirit. Our need today is to turn to this spirit and remain there, enthroning the Lord. Then in a very practical way our spirit will be joined to the third heaven. We shall realize in our experience that, on the one hand, the Holy of Holies is in heaven and that, on the other hand, it is also in our spirit. This indicates that when we remain in our spirit, we actually touch the heavens. If we enthrone the Lord Jesus within us, the Spirit as the water of life will flow from the throne to supply us. This is grace, and this is the way to receive grace and enjoy grace. (*Life-study of Galatians,* pp. 328-330)

Isaac also became the heir in grace (Gen. 21:9-12). All that his father had was his, for Abraham gave all his riches to this unique heir. Likewise, we should have no enjoyment in ourselves. All the enjoyment of the inheritance must be in grace. (*Life-study of Genesis,* p. 833)

Further Reading: Life-study of Galatians, msg. 37; *CWWN,* vol. 35, "The God of Abraham, Isaac, and Jacob," ch. 8

Enlightenment and inspiration: _____

_____

_____

_____

Morning Nourishment

Gen.
24:36
And Sarah my master's wife bore a son to my master after she had become old. And he has given all that he has to him.

22:9 And they came to the place of which God had told him. And Abraham built the altar there and laid the wood in order and bound Isaac his son and laid him on the altar on top of the wood.

Isaac inherited all things from his father (Gen. 24:36; 25:5). It was by grace, not by his effort, that he became the heir of the father's riches. He was not required to do anything that he might inherit the father's riches, and he did not do anything for the inheritance. It was absolutely and unconditionally of grace.

In the New Testament, all the called believers are heirs of God's absolute and unconditional grace. God has called us and has blessed us with all the spiritual blessings in Christ (Eph. 1:3). In Christ He has put us into grace that we might become the heirs of grace, inheriting all the riches of the divine fullness as our enjoyment. Our Christian life must be like Isaac's, doing nothing by himself, but inheriting and enjoying all that the father has. In the inheriting of grace, we must cease from the effort of our natural life that we may keep ourselves open and available for the enjoyment of grace. (*Life-study of Genesis,* pp. 833-834)

Today's Reading

Isaac also obeyed in grace (Gen. 22:5-10). In my reading of Genesis 22 in the past, I could not understand how Isaac, a young man, could have been so obedient. Eventually, I saw that he was obedient because he was saturated with grace. He was absolutely in grace, and his obedience was also in grace. That obedience brought in God's provision. It is the same with us today. Whenever we obey in grace, we shall meet the provision of God.

God's grace is powerful, enabling us to bear anything. Paul told Timothy to "be empowered in the grace" of Christ (2 Tim. 2:1). Grace can even reign over all things (Rom. 5:21). We should not fall from grace (Gal. 5:4) but rather be confirmed by it (Heb. 13:9). The more we bear in grace, the more provision of grace we meet and participate in.

[Genesis 26:13 says that] Isaac "became rich and continued to grow richer until he became very rich." He became rich by fulfilling the regular duty of sowing and through the Lord's blessing. This also was a matter of enjoyment, but this enjoyment was not on the proper standing. Isaac might have said to himself, "My standing must be right. If it were not right, how could the Lord have blessed me with all these riches?" But God might have said, "Isaac, you are settled here and have gained great riches, but I do not agree with your standing. I shall raise up the circumstances to force you to leave this place." May the Holy Spirit show us such a vivid picture here. On the one hand, there is the proper enjoyment; on the other hand, there is the improper standing. Even if we lack the proper standing, we may continue to have the enjoyment. But do not think that this enjoyment justifies your standing. As long as we have the enjoyment, our need is met. But for the fulfillment of God's eternal purpose, we need to get on the proper standing. Nevertheless, even if we are not on the proper standing, God still grants us His rich provision. This is wonderful. What a wonderful God! What a wonderful provision! We have been destined for the enjoyment. Even when we are wrong in our standing, we may still have the rich enjoyment. But God will not let us go. He will use our circumstances to bring us back to the proper standing that the fulfillment of His purpose might be realized.

Before Isaac came back to Beer-sheba, he had enjoyment after enjoyment, grace upon grace. After receiving the hundred-fold harvest, he found the "well of springing water" and came into the "broad places," the "broad ways" (Rehoboth, 26:15-22). Although he had enjoyment in such a rich way, his standing was not right and he was forced to leave the broad ways and to come back to Beer-sheba. (*Life-study of Genesis,* pp. 833, 845-846)

Further Reading: Life-study of Genesis, msg. 63

Enlightenment and inspiration: _____

_____
_____
_____

Morning Nourishment

Gen. And Jehovah appeared to him the same night and
26:24-25 said, I am the God of Abraham your father. Do not
be afraid, for I am with you, and I will bless you
and multiply your seed for My servant Abraham's
sake. And he built an altar there and called upon
the name of Jehovah and pitched his tent there.
And there Isaac's servants dug a well.

Although Isaac enjoyed God's unconditional grace, finding
enjoyment and satisfaction (signified by a well) in every place
that he went (Gen. 25:11; 26:15-22), Beer-sheba was the unique
place in which he experienced God's appearing, received His
promise, built an altar, called on the name of the Lord, and
pitched a tent as a testimony. God's called ones are destined to
enjoy God's grace regardless of their standing, but this enjoyment does not justify their standing. If we desire to have God's
appearing, inherit His promises, and live a life for the fulfillment
of His eternal purpose, we must come to the unique place that
God has chosen and remain there. This unique place is signified
by Beer-sheba, with the well for life supply and the tamarisk
tree as the expression of the rich flow of life (21:25, 33). Cf. footnotes 1 on Deuteronomy 12:5 and 17. (Gen. 26:24, footnote 1)

Today's Reading

Isaac was a very restful person. In spite of the troubles he en-
countered with the Philistines over the wells, he was always at rest.
Although Isaac faced some troubles, he himself was not troubled.

When some hear that Isaac had a well wherever he went,
they may think that, since this enjoyment is also their destiny,
they may go wherever they want. Do not think like this. You may
have a well for your enjoyment, but you will miss the Lord's
appearing and be unable to fulfill God's eternal purpose....God's
purpose can never be fulfilled in Lahai-roi, Esek, Sitnah, or even
in Rehoboth. It can only be fulfilled in Beer-sheba, and we must
remain there. If we do, we shall experience the Lord's appearing
and have the ground to inherit the promises to fulfill God's

eternal purpose. Although we may have wells, even "a well of living water" (Gen. 26:19, Heb.), in other places, those wells cannot enable us to fulfill God's eternal purpose. His purpose can only be fulfilled at the well near the tamarisk tree in Beer-sheba.

Although Isaac had some enjoyment at every place where there was a well, God was not satisfied and used the environment to force Isaac to return to Beer-sheba. God seemed to say, "Isaac, you are settled, but you are not settled in the right place. I shall stir up contention that will force you to go back to Beer-sheba."

When Isaac returned to Beer-sheba (26:23-33), the Lord immediately appeared to him, speaking to him and confirming His promise [v. 24]....In Beer-sheba Isaac began to have the proper testimony. He built an altar, called upon the name of the Lord, and pitched his tent (26:25). Here in Beer-sheba he had a life for the fulfillment of God's eternal purpose. Eventually, here in Beer-sheba the opposers were subdued (26:26-31). Beer-sheba is the right place, the place where we can have the proper standing, and the proper standing means a great deal both to God and to us.

Isaac inherited not only all that his father had, but also the promise which God had given to his father concerning the good land and the unique seed, which is Christ in whom all the nations of the earth will be blessed (26:3-5). This promise was actually for the fulfillment of God's purpose that God might have a kingdom on the earth in which to express Himself through a corporate people. Both the good land and the seed are for the formation of a kingdom for God on the earth. In this kingdom God can be fully expressed in the seed, into which He will work Himself and which will be transformed into His image. This was a promise given to Abraham and inherited by Isaac. But it is a fulfillment with us today. Today we are enjoying the Triune God as our grace. Through our enjoyment of grace the kingdom of God will be realized and God in Christ will be fully expressed for eternity. (*Life-study of Genesis,* pp. 837, 841-842, 846, 834)

Further Reading: Life-study of Genesis, msg. 64

Enlightenment and inspiration: _____

_____
_____
_____

Hymns, #395

1 O Jesus Christ, grow Thou in me,
     And all things else recede;
  My heart be daily nearer Thee,
     From sin be daily freed.

     Each day let Thy supporting might
       My weakness still embrace;
     My darkness vanish in Thy light,
       Thy life my death efface.

2 In Thy bright beams which on me fall,
     Fade every evil thought;
  That I am nothing, Thou art all,
     I would be daily taught.

3 More of Thy glory let me see,
     Thou Holy, Wise, and True;
  I would Thy living image be,
     In joy and sorrow too.

4 Fill me with gladness from above,
     Hold me by strength divine;
  Lord, let the glow of Thy great love
     Through all my being shine.

5 Make this poor self grow less and less,
     Be Thou my life and aim;
  Oh, make me daily through Thy grace
     More meet to bear Thy name.

Composition for prophecy with main point and sub-points: _____

_____
_____
_____
_____
_____
_____
_____
_____
_____
_____
_____
_____
_____
_____
_____
_____
_____
_____
_____
_____
_____
_____
_____
_____
_____
_____
_____
_____
_____
_____
_____
_____
_____
_____
_____

Two Wells—Two Sources of Living

Scripture Reading: Gen. 21:15-34

Day 1 I. **A well signifies the source of one's living; the two wells in Genesis 21:15-34 signify two sources of living:**

A. One well is the natural source in the wilderness of our soul; this source is represented by Ishmael, who lived in the wilderness and was joined to Egypt (vv. 19-21).

B. The other well is the redeemed source in the garden of our spirit; this source is represented by Isaac, who lived at Beer-sheba and was brought to Mount Moriah (vv. 25, 31; cf. 22:2).

C. Today there are two kinds of Christians:

1. One kind is like Ishmael, living for themselves in the wilderness of their soul and being joined to the world (1 John 2:15-17).

2. The other kind is like Isaac, living for God in their spirit and in the church life and being brought to Zion (Rom. 8:4; 12:4-5; 16:1; Rev. 14:1).

3. Even we, real Christians, may be like Ishmael, living in and for ourselves and being joined to the world, unless, as typified by Isaac, we live in our spirit and in the church life so that we might reach God's goal (21:2; 22:16a).

II. **Ishmael's well, the source of his living, was in the wilderness, a place rejected by God (Gen. 21:19-21; 25:12, 18):**

A. Ishmael's well, the source of his living, made him an archer (21:20):

1. An archer is a wild hunter like Nimrod in 10:8-12, a killer in the wilderness.

2. If we stay in the wilderness of our soul and drink water out of the well for Ishmael, the source of his living, we will be made an

archer using the bow to kill life for building up our own kingdom, not a planter growing life for the building up of God's kingdom.

B. Ishmael's well, the source of his living, joined him to Egypt, to the world (21:21):

　　1. Hagar took a wife for Ishmael from Egypt, her own source, sealing him with the things of Egypt.

　　2. There is a well, a source of living, that can make us a wild hunter who kills life and that can join us to the world.

Day 2 & Day 3

III. **Isaac's well, the source of his living, was in Beer-sheba (vv. 25, 31):**

A. Many verses in the Bible refer to this well, the divine source:

　　1. At Elim "there were twelve springs of water and seventy palm trees" (Exo. 15:27):

　　　　a. In the Bible a spring signifies life that flows out of God in resurrection (John 4:10, 14; 7:37-39; Rev. 22:1).

　　　　b. Palm trees signify life that is flourishing, rejoicing in satisfaction, and victorious over tribulation (Psa. 92:12; Lev. 23:40; Neh. 8:15; John 12:13; Rev. 7:9).

　　2. "Then Israel sang this song: Spring up, O well! Sing to it! / The well, which the leaders sank, / Which the nobles of the people dug, / With the scepter, with their staffs" (Num. 21:17-18):

　　　　a. The well here at Beer typifies Christ within us (v. 16; John 4:11-12, 14).

　　　　b. The digging of the well signifies the digging away of the "dirt," the barriers in our heart—our mind, emotion, will, and conscience—so that the Spirit as the living water may spring up within us and flow freely (cf. Gen. 26:15, 18).

　　3. "A fountain in gardens, / A well of living water, / And streams from Lebanon" (S. S. 4:15):

a. The fountain in gardens and the well of living water of the life-giving Spirit are streams from the resurrection and ascension life (Lebanon, v. 8) (John 7:38-39).

b. The fountain and the spring stream out from the overcomers, flowing out from what they are and from where they are.

B. The well for Isaac was a redeemed well (Gen. 21:28-32):

1. Abraham redeemed this well at the cost of seven ewe lambs.

2. In typology these lambs signify the full redemption of Christ, indicating that the divine living water has been redeemed, bought back, by Christ's full redemption (Eph. 1:7; 1 Pet. 1:18-19; John 19:34):

a. Today the whole human race is living by a source that is without redemption; we are living by a redeemed source.

b. The living water that we are drinking today is not natural; it is water that has been redeemed at a great cost.

C. The well for Isaac also needed a covenant (Gen. 21:31-32):

1. The covenant here, involving the redeeming of the well at Beer-sheba, is a seed of the new covenant, enacted through Christ's redeeming blood (Matt. 26:28; Luke 22:20; Heb. 8:8-13).

2. Isaac drank of redeemed water, the water of the covenant; likewise, the living water that the New Testament believers drink today is redeemed and covenanted water (John 4:14; Heb. 8:10-13).

Day 4 IV. **"Abraham planted a tamarisk tree in Beer-sheba, and there he called on the name of Jehovah, the Eternal God" (Gen. 21:33):**

A. As the tree of life is the center of Genesis 2, the tamarisk tree is the center of Genesis 21:

    1. A tamarisk tree, having slender branches and very fine leaves, portrays the flow of the riches of life, the issue of the experience of the tree of life; thus, the tamarisk tree signifies the tree of life experienced and expressed (2:9-10).

    2. The fact that Abraham planted a tamarisk tree after making the covenant for the well at Beer-sheba indicates that the water of which he drank was flowing in a rich way (21:32-33; cf. John 7:37-39).

    3. The church life today is by the well in Beer-sheba; when we drink of this water and live by it, we will be like a tamarisk tree flowing with the riches of life:

       a. The church should be at the well of an oath with a covenant and should also be full of tamarisk trees, the tree of life experienced by us (1:4; 10:10).

       b. Our Christian life and the proper church life are both a tamarisk tree, expressing the tree of life by which we live (6:57b).

Day 5 B. There in Beer-sheba by the tamarisk tree Abraham called on the name of Jehovah, the Eternal God (Gen. 21:33):

    1. Here we have a special title of God—*Jehovah, El Olam*; *El* means "the Mighty One," and *Olam*, meaning "eternal" or "eternity," comes from a Hebrew root meaning "to conceal," "to hide":

       a. Abraham experienced God as the Eternal One, as the secret and mysterious One.

       b. God's existence is eternal, for He has neither beginning nor ending; He is the Eternal God (Psa. 90:2; Isa. 40:28).

       c. The divine title *El Olam* implies eternal life (1 John 1:2; 2:25; 5:11-13).

    2. In Genesis 21 Abraham experienced God as the eternal life, as the divine person who is

concealed, veiled, hidden, mysterious, secret, and yet real, ever-existing, and ever-
living, without beginning or ending (Exo.
3:14; John 3:16):

Day 6

a. The eternal life is the life "which is really
   life" (1 Tim. 6:19b).
b. Life is the Triune God dispensed into us
   and living in us:
   (1) God the Father is the source of life
       (John 5:26), God the Son is the em-
       bodiment of life (1:4), and God the
       Spirit is the flow of life (4:14b).
   (2) God the Father is the light of life
       (Rev. 21:23; 22:5), God the Son is
       the tree of life (v. 2), and God the
       Spirit is the river of life (v. 1).
c. The eternal life, which is the Son, not
   only was with the Father but also was
   living and acting in communion with the
   Father in eternity (1 John 1:1-2; John
   1:1-2).
d. The eternal life was manifested to the
   apostles, who saw, testified, and reported
   this life to people; the manifestation of
   the eternal life includes the revelation
   and impartation of life to men, with a
   view to bringing man into the eternal
   life, into its union and communion with
   the Father (1 John 1:1-3).
e. The eternal life was promised by God,
   released through Christ's death, and imparted to the believers through Christ's
   resurrection (2:25; John 3:14-15; 12:24;
   cf. Luke 12:49-50; 1 Pet. 1:3).
f. The eternal life was received by the believers through believing in the Son; after
   the believers receive eternal life, this
   life becomes their life (John 3:15-16, 36a;
   Col. 3:4a; John 1:12-13).

Morning Nourishment

Rom. That the righteous requirement of the law might
8:4 be fulfilled in us, who do not walk according to the
flesh but according to the spirit.
1 John Do not love the world nor the things in the world.
2:15 If anyone loves the world, love for the Father is not
in him.

Out of Abraham two kinds of people came into existence. One
is represented by Ishmael who lived in the wilderness and who
was joined to Egypt; the other is represented by Isaac who lived
at Beer-sheba and who was brought to Mount Moriah. Today
there are also two kinds of Christians. One kind is like Ishmael,
living for themselves in the wilderness of their soul and being
joined to the world. The other kind is like Isaac, living for God
in their spirit and in the church and being brought to Zion.
Even we, the real Christians, may be like Ishmael, living in and
for ourselves and being joined to the world, unless, as typified
by Isaac, we live in our spirit and in the church that we might
reach God's goal. (*Life-study of Genesis,* p. 751)

Today's Reading

[The two wells in Genesis 21:15-34 signify two sources of
living.] The source from which Ishmael drank made him an
archer, one who lived wildly for himself. But Isaac's source of
living made him a burnt offering, one who was offered to God for
His satisfaction [22:2, 9].

This source of living led Isaac up to Moriah, not down to
Egypt (22:2). Ishmael's source of living leads people downward,
but Isaac's source leads people upward to the mountain in
Moriah where Jerusalem was later built. This going up to
Moriah kept God's people from the Philistines. We also need to
go up from Beer-sheba to Jerusalem, not only having the church
life at Beer-sheba but also in Jerusalem. Ultimately, this proper
source of life will make all of us Isaacs and will lead us to the
New Jerusalem.

Here we have another seed of the divine revelation. Ishmael

lived in the wilderness and was joined to Egypt, but Isaac lived in a planted place and was led to Moriah. The mountain in Moriah eventually became Mount Zion upon which God's temple was built (2 Chron. 3:1), thus becoming the center of the good land that God gave to Abraham and his descendants. After his descendants followed the way of Ishmael and went down to Egypt, God brought them out of that land with the intention of bringing them into the good land of Canaan. But their unbelief kept them wandering in the wilderness where Ishmael lived. Eventually, God brought their children into the good land and chose Jerusalem, which was built on Mount Moriah, as the unique center for them to worship Him.

Ishmael's well, the source of his living, was in the wilderness close to Egypt (Gen. 21:19-21; 25:12, 18). In the Bible, the wilderness always represents a place rejected by God. God never accepts the wilderness. As long as we are in the wilderness, we are rejected by Him. The best illustration of this is the wandering in the wilderness by the children of Israel. In figure, the wilderness also signifies our soul. If we live in our soul, we are straying in the wilderness that is rejected by God. The wilderness where Ishmael's well was located was close to Egypt. He could easily drift from there into Egypt. This means that when we are in our soul, in our natural being, we are wandering in the wilderness and can easily drift into the world.

Ishmael's source of living eventually joined him to Egypt, that is, to the world (21:21). When Hagar took a wife for Ishmael, she took a wife from Egypt, from her own source. Being an Egyptian, she desired to have an Egyptian woman as her daughter-in-law. By taking a wife out of the land of Egypt for Ishmael, Hagar sealed him with the things of Egypt. We see from all this that there is a well, a source of living, that can make us a wild hunter who kills life and that can join us to the world. (*Life-study of Genesis*, pp. 750-751, 744-745)

Further Reading: Life-study of Genesis, msgs. 46, 56

Enlightenment and inspiration: _____

_____

_____

_____

Morning Nourishment

Gen.   And he said, These seven ewe lambs you shall take
21:30-32 from my hand, that it may be a witness for me that
        I dug this well. Therefore he called that place Beer-
        sheba, because there the two of them swore an
        oath. So they made a covenant at Beer-sheba...
Luke   And similarly the cup after they had dined, saying,
22:20 This cup is the new covenant *established* in My
        blood, which is being poured out for you.

Praise the Lord that there is another well—the well for
Isaac (Gen. 21:22-34). Many verses in the Bible speak of this
positive well. Psalm 36:8 says, "You cause them to drink of the
river of Your pleasures." The Lord likes to make us drink of His
river of pleasures. In John 4:14 the Lord Jesus said, "Whoever
drinks of the water that I will give him shall by no means thirst
forever; but the water that I will give him will become in him a
fountain of water springing up into eternal life." This means
that God Himself will be our life. In John 7:37 and 38 the Lord
Jesus also spoke of drinking: "If anyone thirsts, let him come to
Me and drink. He who believes into Me, as the Scripture said,
out of his innermost being shall flow rivers of living water."
Moreover, in 1 Corinthians 12:13, the apostle Paul says that we
have all been made to drink of one Spirit, that is, of one well of
water. Even the last chapter of the Bible contains a word about
drinking: "And the Spirit and the bride say, Come!...Let him
who is thirsty come; let him who wills take the water of life
freely" (Rev. 22:17). This divine well must be the source of our
living. (*Life-study of Genesis*, pp. 745-746)

Today's Reading

Although Christ has been brought forth and has grown up,
in the church life we still must learn that there are two sources
or two kinds of living. What kind of living do you have—the
living of Ishmael or the living of Isaac? It is insufficient merely
to say that you have the living of Isaac. You must examine the
kind of water you are drinking day by day. Are you drinking of

the well for Ishmael? If you are, that well will make you an Ishmael and will cause you to drift into the world. Are you drinking of the well for Isaac, the well which signifies the divine well, the well of Christ, the well of the Spirit? If you are drinking of this well, the divine water which flows out of it will accomplish a great deal.

The well for Isaac was a redeemed well (Gen. 21:28-30). This well, which Abraham had dug, was lost, having been violently taken away by Abimelech's servants (v. 25). Then Abraham redeemed it at the cost of seven ewe lambs. In typology, these lambs signify the full redemption of Christ, indicating that the divine living water has been redeemed, bought back, by Christ's full redemption. Today, while the whole human race is living by a source which is without redemption, we are living by a redeemed source. The living water which we are drinking today is not natural; it has been redeemed at the cost of Christ's complete redemption.

The well for Isaac also needed a covenant (vv. 31-32). The covenant here is a seed of the new covenant. Our living water today is not only redeemed water but also covenanted water. Ishmael drank of wild water, water that was without redemption and covenant. But all the water which Isaac drank was redeemed water, the water of the covenant. Since we have begun to know Christ, the source of our living has also been the redeemed and covenanted water.

In this section of the Word it is clearly revealed that there are two sources of living. One is the natural source in the wilderness of our soul, whereas the other is the redeemed source in the garden of our spirit. At Beer-sheba, Abraham was contending for the well which had been so violently taken away. Today we also need to fight for the divine well that we may have it for both the Christian life and the proper church life. (*Life-study of Genesis,* pp. 746-748)

Further Reading: Life-study of Genesis, msg. 46

__Enlightenment and inspiration:__ _____

_____

_____

_____

Morning Nourishment

Num. **Then Israel sang this song: Spring up, O well! Sing**
21:17-18 **to it! The well, which the leaders sank, which the**
nobles of the people dug, with the scepter, with
their staffs...

In Numbers 20 the smitten rock, which typifies Christ as
smitten and riven, flowed with living water (cf. 1 Cor. 10:4). Then
in Numbers 21 the well dug by the people of God sprang up with
water. Therefore, in these two chapters of [Numbers] there is
first a rock that must be smitten for the living water to flow out
and then a well that must be dug for the water to spring up.

Both the rock and the well are types of Christ, revealing Him
in two different aspects. The rock typifies Christ on the cross,
smitten by God so that the living water, which is the Spirit of life,
may flow out into us. The well shows a different aspect. Whereas
the rock is Christ on the cross, the well is Christ within us (John
4:14). For believers, it is not a matter of the rock but the well.
Christ as the rock has already accomplished His work on the
cross, which issued in the water of life flowing into us, but today
Christ as the well of living water springing up continuously
within us is something else and has much to do with the present
process of digging. (*The Economy of God,* p. 91)

Today's Reading

Even up to the present moment most of us do not have the free
flow of living water. Our prayers are not so free, our testimonies are
not so strong, and in many ways we have been defeated and are not
so victorious. This is due to one thing: the flow of the spiritual life,
or the spring of the living water, is not free within us. There is much
dirt within us that must be dug out. You may ask, "What is this
dirt?" It is the dirt in our conscience, our emotion, our will, and our
mind. Our heart has much dirt, which needs to be dug out, and
even in our spirit there is some dirt, which must be dealt with.

If we would experience a free, inward flow of the Spirit, our
conscience must first be dealt with and purified. The dirt can only
be dug away by going to the Lord several times each day. I would

suggest that during this week we go to the Lord again and again, even while we are walking along the street. We have to go to the Lord in our spirit and be dug in His presence. By the help of the Holy Spirit we must dig away all the dirt.

After dealing with the accusations in our conscience, we must also dig away the many things condemned by the Lord in our heart. Not many brothers and sisters have a pure heart in seeking only the Lord Himself. On one hand, many are seeking the Lord and His way, but on the other, they are still seeking too many things other than the Lord Himself. The heart then becomes complicated and is not free and pure. We must go to the Lord once again to dig away all the things other than Christ in our heart.

Seek the Lord's presence, and ask Him to bring you into His light. Then follow His light....The more you dig away the dirt, the more you will be alive....You must maintain the flow of living water, that is, the fellowship of life flowing freely within you. When the living water flows freely within you, then there is victory. All the problems will be solved spontaneously and even unconsciously....This flowing of the living water is entirely dependent upon your digging.

This digging is accomplished only by prayer. We have to spend more and more time with the Lord and pray according to His inner leading. According to that leading, we must confess and dig away all the dirt within us....Sometimes we need to pray with others, but the digging prayer is more prevailing in privacy. It is extremely necessary to spend more private time with the Lord. All the dirt within the conscience, heart, mind, will, and emotion must be dug away by our prayers. You may say, "I am so busy." But although we are busy with the duties of the day, we can still touch the Lord and dig away the dirt. Many times while I am working, I apply myself to the digging exercise. We should learn to pray, to contact the Lord, and to dig away all the inward dirt. (*The Economy of God,* pp. 91-93, 96)

Further Reading: The Economy of God, ch. 10

Enlightenment and inspiration: _____

_____

_____

_____

Morning Nourishment

Gen. **And Abraham planted a tamarisk tree in Beer-**
21:33 **sheba, and there he called on the name of Jehovah,**
the Eternal God.
John **...I have come that they may have life and may**
10:10 **have *it* abundantly.**
6:57 **As the living Father has sent Me and I live because**
of the Father, so he who eats Me, he also shall live
because of Me.

In Beer-sheba Abraham planted a tamarisk tree (Gen. 21:33). A tamarisk, a type of willow tree, has very fine leaves, often grows near water, and gives the impression of the flowing of the riches of life. That Abraham planted a tamarisk after making the covenant for the well at Beer-sheba indicates that the water of which he drank was flowing in a rich way. The Lord Jesus said that whoever believes in Him will have rivers of living water flowing out of his innermost being.

When you drink of this well and live by it, you will be like a tamarisk flowing with the riches of life. Whenever people come to you, they will never sense dryness but will be refreshed by the water of life. Beer-sheba, which means "the well of an oath," is the place where the church should be. The church should be at the well of an oath with a covenant and should also be full of tamarisk trees. We all need to be a flowing tamarisk....Praise the Lord that there are some real tamarisks in the local churches! (*Life-study of Genesis,* pp. 747-748)

Today's Reading

The center of the revelation in Genesis 2 is the tree of life. Likewise, the center of the revelation in the second part of Genesis 21 is the tamarisk tree. If we have the spiritual realization with the divine light, we shall see that the tamarisk tree here is the tree of life experienced and expressed. When the tree of life is not experienced or expressed by us, it is simply the tree of life. But once we experience and express it, it becomes a tamarisk tree. A tamarisk tree has slender branches and very fine leaves showing the flow of the riches of life. Thus, the tamarisk tree planted by the well of an oath in Beer-sheba pictures the flow of the riches of life, the issue of the experience of the tree of life. Is the tree of life a tamarisk tree in your experience? Whenever we come to the meetings, the tree of life must become a tamarisk tree.

With Ishmael there was not a tree flowing with the riches of life; there was a bow. While the sign of Ishmael's life was a life-killing bow, the sign of Isaac's life was a life-flowing tree. As a Christian, a child of God and a descendant of Abraham, what is your sign—a bow or a tamarisk tree? Are you killing life, or is life with all its riches flowing in you?

According to our opinion, the planting of a tamarisk tree may be insignificant, perhaps being only an ancient type of landscaping. But the Bible connects the planting of the tamarisk tree with calling on a new title of the Lord, the Eternal God. Notice how the conjunction "and" is used to connect these two items in 21:33. Abraham planted a tamarisk tree and there called on the name of Jehovah, El Olam. According to our human thought, planting a tree is unrelated to calling on the name of the Lord, especially to such a new and recently revealed title. But in the Bible here it gives us the ground for the proper calling on the Lord. If we would call on the name of the Lord, we need a tamarisk tree. If we do not have this tamarisk tree experience, we can only call on the old title of God, Jehovah, not on His newly unveiled title, El Olam.

We need to consider our own experience. Whenever we have had the flow of the riches of the divine life, that was the time when we called on the name of the Lord Jesus with a new realization. We called on the same Lord, but in our calling we had a fresh sense. Do you think that if you held the life-killing bow in your hand, you would be able to call on the Lord's name? No, rather you would go to find an Egyptian wife. (*Life-study of Genesis,* pp. 753-755)

Further Reading: Life-study of Genesis, mgs. 56-57

Enlightenment and inspiration: _____

_____

_____

_____

Morning Nourishment

Gen. And Abraham planted a tamarisk tree in Beer-
21:33 sheba, and there he called on the name of Jehovah,
the Eternal God.
Psa. ...Indeed from eternity to eternity, You are God.
90:2
1 John And this is the testimony, that God gave to us eter-
5:11 nal life and this life is in His Son.

Genesis 21:33, which tells us that Abraham planted a tamarisk tree in Beer-sheba, also says that "there he called on the
name of Jehovah, the Eternal God." Here we see another special
title of God—Jehovah, El Olam....The Hebrew word *olam* means
eternity or eternal. However, the root of this Hebrew word means
to conceal, hide, or veil from sight. Anything which is veiled spontaneously becomes secret. Abraham eventually experienced God
as the Eternal One, as the secret and mysterious One. We cannot
see or touch Him, yet He is so real. His existence is eternal, for He
has neither beginning nor ending. He is the Eternal God (Psa.
90:2; Isa. 40:28). (*Life-study of Genesis,* pp. 748-749)

Today's Reading

[In Genesis 21] we find another seed which is developed in the
New Testament. The God whom Abraham experienced in chapter 21 is the same as the One revealed in John 1:1, 4: "In the beginning was the Word,...and the Word was God....In Him was life."
This life is the very El Olam. The mysterious God in eternity is
our eternal life. Eternal life is a divine person who is so concealed,
veiled, hidden, mysterious, secret, and yet so real, ever-existing,
and ever-living, without beginning or ending. The title El Olam
implies eternal life. Here God was not revealed to Abraham but
was experienced by him as the ever-living, secret, mysterious One
who is the eternal life. In other words, in Genesis 21 Abraham
experienced God as the eternal life. By the tamarisk tree in Beer-
sheba, Abraham could testify to the whole universe that he was
experiencing the hidden, ever-living One as his mysterious life.
There, at Beer-sheba, he called on the name of Jehovah, El Olam.

In chapter 12 he only called upon the name of Jehovah, not yet experiencing Him as the God who is the mysterious, ever-living One. But here in chapter 21, after having so much experience, with Isaac at Beer-sheba under the tamarisk tree he experienced the ever-living, mysterious One as his inner life and called, "O Jehovah, El Olam!" Although no one could see this mysterious One, He was real to Abraham in his experience. The One we have within us today is the very El Olam, the hidden, secret, concealed, mysterious, ever-living One. He is our life. We may have the same enjoyment Abraham had simply by calling, "O Lord Jesus."

While Abraham was sojourning in Beer-sheba, he must have done many things. But here the Scripture only tells us of one thing—that Abraham planted a tamarisk tree at Beer-sheba and called on the name of Jehovah, El Olam. By this brief record we can see two things. One is that the planting of the tamarisk tree must have been very significant; the other is that this planting of the tamarisk tree is connected with calling on the name of Jehovah, El Olam. As we have pointed out, Genesis 1 and 2 are not merely a record of God's creation but a record of life, with the tree of life as its center. Likewise this section of the Word is not merely a record of Abraham's history; it also is a record of life, showing by what source Abraham was living. He lived by calling on Jehovah, El Olam, by experiencing the eternal, hidden God as his life. In New Testament terms, he was experiencing the eternal life flowing with all its riches like a tamarisk tree which expresses the riches of the well by which it lives. As the tree of life is the center of the record in chapters 1 and 2, the tamarisk tree is the center of the record here. We may say that the tamarisk tree is the tree of life experienced by us. It is the expression of the tree of life. Our Christian life and the proper church life are both a tamarisk tree, expressing the tree of life by which we live. This goes together with the calling on the Lord who is our eternal life, our Jehovah, El Olam. (*Life-study of Genesis,* pp. 749-750)

Further Reading: Life-study of Genesis, msgs. 56-57

Enlightenment and inspiration: _____
_____
_____

Morning Nourishment

1 John (And the life was manifested, and we have seen
  1:2   and testify and report to you the eternal life, which
        was with the Father and was manifested to us).
John   He who believes into the Son has eternal life; but
  3:36 he who disobeys the Son shall not see life...
Col.   When Christ our life is manifested, then you also
  3:4   will be manifested with Him in glory.

Eternal life is the life of God (Eph. 4:18; 2 Pet. 1:3). We may say that this life is actually God Himself with the contents of divine love and divine light. And this life is of the Spirit of God (Rom. 8:2), especially when it becomes our life for our enjoyment.

Eternal life is also the Son of God. This life is not simply a matter or a thing; this life is a person. The divine life is God Himself expressed in His Son. First John 5:12 says, "He who has the Son has the life." In our experience we know that eternal life is the Son of God Himself. (*Life-study of 1 John*, p. 35)

Today's Reading

First John 1:2 says that eternal life was with the Father. The Greek word rendered "with" is *pros* (used with the Greek accusative case). It is a preposition of motion, implying living, acting, in union and communion with. The eternal life which is the Son was not only with the Father but was living and acting in union and communion with the Father in eternity....The Father is the source of the eternal life, from whom and with whom the Son was manifested as the expression of the eternal life for those the Father has chosen to partake of and enjoy this life.

Instead of trying to analyze these aspects of eternal life, we should enjoy them as "courses" of a spiritual meal. Eternal life is the life of God, it is the Son of God, and it was with the Father in eternity. Here we have at least four courses for our enjoyment: God, the Son of God, the Father, and eternity.

According to my experience, the best way to enjoy [these marvelous courses] is to pray-read the Word. For example, pray-read the words "the life of God" found in Ephesians 4:18. As you pray-read, you may say, "Oh, the life of God! Amen! Right now, I enjoy God, and I enjoy Him as my life. Hallelujah for God! Hallelujah for life! Hallelujah for the life of God! Hallelujah for the enjoyment of the life of God and for the enjoyment of God as life!"

John says that the life which was with the Father was manifested to the apostles. The manifestation of eternal life includes revelation and impartation of life to men, with a view to bringing man into the eternal life, into its union and communion with the Father. What was once hidden has been manifested to the apostles. John, one of the apostles, now opens to us the divine mysteries. If we eat the Word through pray-reading, we shall receive the benefit of the manifestation of eternal life.

Eternal life was not only promised and manifested; it was also released through Christ's death (John 3:14-15). The divine life was concealed, confined, in Christ. But through His death this divine life was released from within Him.

The eternal life that was released from within Christ through His death has been imparted into the believers through His resurrection. Concerning this, 1 Peter 1:3 says, "Blessed be the God and Father of our Lord Jesus Christ, who according to His great mercy has regenerated us unto a living hope through the resurrection of Jesus Christ from the dead."

The eternal life that has been released through Christ's death and imparted through His resurrection has been received by the believers through their believing in the Son. According to John 3:15-16 and 36, everyone who believes in the Son has eternal life.

After the believers receive eternal life, this life becomes their life (Col. 3:4). This is the purpose of God's salvation, that is, to make His life our life so that we may become His children, partaking of His divine nature to enjoy all that He is and to live a life that expresses Him. (*Life-study of 1 John,* pp. 35-37)

Further Reading: Life-study of 1 John, msg. 4; *Basic Lessons on Life,* lsns. 7, 13; *Knowing Life and the Church,* chs. 1-2; *Knowing and Experiencing God as Life,* chs. 2-4

Enlightenment and inspiration: _____

_____

_____

_____

Hymns, #602

1   O how glorious! O how holy!
      God is the eternal life!
    Full, unlimited, and pow'rful,
      Pure, and merciful, and bright!
    In this life are all His riches,
      All His nature, love and light.

2   O how loving! O how gracious!
      God Himself is life to man!
    He in man hath made a spirit
      That He might fulfill His plan.
    'Tis His heart's delight and longing
      E'er to be received by man.

3   O what love and grace unbounded!
      God as life to man doth flow!
    He no more is hid in secret
      But Himself to man doth show,
    First in flesh and then as Spirit
      That His life all men may know.

4   How approachable! How near us!
      God in Christ our life to be!
    Christ is God in flesh incarnate,
      Manifest for man to see.
    Died and risen, now He enters
      Into man, his life to be.

5   O what wonder! As the Spirit
      God as life to man is shown!
    'Tis His other transformation,
      He as Spirit thus is known;
    Men convicting and inspiring,
      He within them makes His home.

6   O how glorious! O how precious!
      Thus the triune God to know!
    First the Father in the Son came,
      Now the Son as Spirit flows.
    When in man the Spirit enters
      God as life He doth bestow.

7   How mysterious, yet how real!
      God Himself now flows in me!
    In my heart, with me in oneness,
      He has come my life to be.
    Hallelujah! Hallelujah!
      I will praise unceasingly!

Composition for prophecy with main point and sub-points: _____

_____

_____

_____

_____

_____

_____

_____

_____

_____

_____

_____

_____

_____

_____

_____

_____

_____

_____

_____

_____

The Offering of Isaac
and Experiencing God
as the One Who Gives Life to the Dead

Scripture Reading: Gen. 22:1-18; Heb. 11:17-19; Rom. 4:17

Day 1   I. **God tested Abraham by instructing him to take his only son, Isaac, and offer him as a burnt offering (Gen. 22:1-2):**
   A. The life at Beer-sheba produces a burnt offering (Isaac) that is offered to God:
      1. Isaac's source of living made him a burnt offering, one who was offered to God for His satisfaction (vv. 2, 7-9):
         a. The Hebrew word for *burnt offering* literally means "that which goes up" and denotes something that ascends to God (Lev. 1:3, footnote 1).
         b. The burnt offering typifies Christ not mainly in His redeeming man from sin but in His living a life that is perfect and absolutely for God and for God's satisfaction and in His being the life that enables God's people to have such a living (v. 9; John 5:19, 30; 6:38; 7:18; 8:29; 14:24; 2 Cor. 5:15; Gal. 2:19-20).
         c. The burnt offering is God's food that God may enjoy it and be satisfied (Num. 28:2).
      2. The proper church life produces burnt offerings (Lev. 1:1-2; Rom. 12:1-2):
         a. The living, growing, and calling on the name of Jehovah, El Olam, at Beer-sheba are all for the producing of a burnt offering (Gen. 21:33; 22:1-2).
         b. The more we stay in the church life, the more it will bring us from Beer-sheba to Moriah.
Day 2   B. Like Abraham, we need to learn the lesson of

offering back to God what He has given to us
(vv. 1-18; Rom. 11:36):

1. Everything concerning Isaac was of God
   and by God, and God required that Abraham
   offer Isaac back to Him as a burnt offering
   (Gen. 22:1-2).
2. Isaac, a type of Christ as the promised seed
   (Gal. 3:16), was given to Abraham by God,
   yet God asked Abraham to give back to God
   what God had given him; this surely was a
   test to Abraham (Gen. 22:1; Heb. 11:17).
3. Here we see a basic principle in God's economy: all that God has given us, even what
   He has wrought into us and through us,
   must eventually be offered back to Him,
   that we may live a life of faith, not holding
   on to anything, even to the things given by
   God, but relying only on Him.
4. The highest demand from God is to give
   back to Him what He has given us.

Day 3 II. **In Genesis 22:1-18 we see Abraham's obedi-
ence of faith (Heb. 11:17-19):**
   A. Abraham did not initiate anything or do any-
      thing according to his concept.
   B. The faith that had been infused into Abraham
      brought him to Mount Moriah, which is another
      name for Mount Zion, and enabled him to offer
      Isaac as a burnt offering (Gen. 22:1-2; 2 Chron. 3:1).

III. **Abraham called the place where he offered
Isaac Jehovah-jireh (Gen. 22:14):**
   A. Moriah means "the vision of Jah," that is, the
      vision of Jehovah; on Mount Moriah Abraham
      saw God, and God saw him (v. 2).
   B. Verse 14b can be translated either, "On the
      mount of Jehovah it will be provided," or "On the
      mount of Jehovah He will be seen":
      1. On Mount Moriah Abraham experienced
         God's provision and received a clear vision.
      2. God's provision is with His vision, so when-

ever we enjoy God's provision, we have a vision
in which we see God, and God sees us.

C. Today God's provision is in the church life, where
we have the full provision with the clear vision.

D. In the Lord's recovery we are journeying upward to Mount Moriah, where we will offer our
Isaac, enjoy God's provision, and have a transparent vision.

Day 4 **IV. After Isaac was offered, he was returned in
resurrection for the fulfillment of God's purpose (vv. 16-18; Heb. 11:17-19; Rom. 4:17):**

A. In receiving Isaac back, Abraham believed in
and experienced God as the One who gives life to
the dead—the God of resurrection (Heb. 11:17-19;
Rom. 4:17; 2 Cor. 1:9).

B. When Isaac was returned in resurrection, he
was no longer a natural Isaac but a resurrected
Isaac.

C. After Isaac was offered, he was returned to
Abraham in resurrection and became a blessing
(Gen. 22:16-18).

D. Everything in our life must pass through the
supreme test of death to make a way for the God
of resurrection (John 11:25; 2 Cor. 1:9).

E. After we offer to God what we have received of
Him, He will return it to us in resurrection (Heb.
11:17-19):

1. Every gift, spiritual blessing, work, and success that we have received of God must pass
through death and eventually be brought
back to us in resurrection.

2. If we offer to God what we have received of
Him and it passes through death, He will
return it to us in resurrection, and it will
become a blessing for the fulfillment of His
purpose (Gen. 22:16-18).

3. God's blessing always comes in resurrection; if we offer our Isaac to God and he is

returned to us in resurrection, we will be under God's blessing.

Day 5   **V. By being offered back to God by Abraham, Isaac was multiplied to become the New Jerusalem (vv. 16-18; Rom. 8:29; Rev. 21:2, 7):**

     A. The New Jerusalem will be the ultimate consummation of Abraham's seed—the sand and the stars (Gen. 22:16-18; Rom. 8:29; Rev. 21:2, 7):

       1. In the New Jerusalem those represented by the twelve tribes are the sand, and those represented by the twelve apostles are the stars (vv. 12, 14).

       2. The two peoples signified by the sand and the stars will be built together into the New Jerusalem.

     B. In Genesis 22 we see a basic principle—that the way to have God's gift multiplied is to offer back to God what He has given to us:

       1. One Isaac, offered to God and returned in resurrection, became numberless stars and sand.

       2. If we offer our one grain to God and allow Him to put it to death, it will be returned to us in resurrection, and we will see multiplication under God's blessing (John 12:24).

Day 6   **VI. Mount Moriah, the place of God's choice, eventually became Mount Zion, the site of the temple and the center of the good land; in our spiritual experience Mount Moriah eventually becomes Mount Zion (Gen. 22:2, 14; 2 Chron. 3:1; Heb. 11:17-19; 12:22-23; Rev. 14:1-5):**

     A. Abraham was the first to worship God with the burnt offering on Mount Zion (v. 1).

     B. Later, Abraham's descendants, the children of Israel, were commanded by God to go three times a year to this place to worship God and there to offer to Him their burnt offerings (Deut. 16:16; Psa. 132:13).

C. Today, Abraham's spiritual descendants, the New Testament believers, are on Mount Zion (Heb. 12:22-23).

D. Eventually, we all will join Abraham to worship God on the eternal Mount Zion, the New Jerusalem; the entire New Jerusalem is Zion, the Holy of Holies, the place where God is (Rev. 14:1-5; 21:22).

E. The Lord's recovery is to build up Zion—the reality of the Body of Christ consummating in the New Jerusalem (14:1; Eph. 4:16; Rev. 21:2).

Morning Nourishment

Gen.   Now after these things God tested Abraham and
22:1-2 said to him, Abraham. And he said, Here I am. And
        He said, Take now your son, your only son, whom
        you love, Isaac, and go to the land of Moriah, and
        offer him there as a burnt offering on one of the
        mountains of which I will tell you.

Do you know that your destiny is to be a burnt offering? To be a
burnt offering is to be killed and burned. The growing, living, and
calling on the name of El Olam at Beer-sheba are all for the building up of a burnt offering that we might be burned on the altar on
Mount Moriah. The water at Beer-sheba is for the fire on Mount
Moriah. The more we drink the water from the well of Beer-
sheba, the more we shall grow, and the more we grow, the more we
shall be prepared for the fire on Mount Moriah. Because of this,
the Lord's recovery will never be a mass movement; it is a narrow
way. At the time of Genesis 22, Isaac was the only person living
and walking in this narrow way. Do not expect that many will
take the way of the church. Many are happy to be a bowman, for
that is a sport. But living at Beer-sheba and calling on the name of
the Lord may seem, in a sense, to be boring. Eventually, after we
enjoy a good time with the Lord, He will ask us to offer our Isaac
to Him. He will not allow us to offer Isaac at Beer-sheba. We shall
have to travel a long distance and climb Mount Moriah. The
proper church life does not produce bowmen; it produces burnt
offerings. We all must become a burnt offering. Although this is a
narrow way, it is prevailing. (*Life-study of Genesis*, p. 759)

Today's Reading

I know of a good number of very brilliant young brothers
who came into the church life with an honest heart. Although
their heart was honest, they expected that one day, after having
all the necessary experiences and receiving all the visions, they
would become something in the Lord's recovery. In other words,
they expected to be spiritual giants. Gradually, as the years
went by, I learned what was on their heart, for they came to me

and told me their story. One brother said, "When I came into the church life, I came in honestly, but I expected that one day, after I had been perfected, equipped, qualified, experienced, and had seen all the visions, I would be so useful in the Lord's hand. But now the Lord has told me that He intends to burn me up." Do you expect that someday you will become a strong bowman? If you do, one day the Lord will say to you, "I don't want an Ishmael, a bowman. I want an Isaac, a burnt offering. Don't try to do anything for Me. I can do anything I want. I just want you to be a burnt offering." The life at Beer-sheba only produces a burnt offering. The more we stay in the church life, the more it will bring us from Beer-sheba to Moriah, from the growing water to the burning fire. Are you growing? Thank God for this. But your growth is a preparation for your being burned. One day we all must pass through the process of being burned as a burnt offering.

In Hebrew the burnt offering means the ascending offering. After the burnt offering has been burned, its sweet odor ascends to God for His satisfaction. It is ascending and not spreading. As a burnt offering, we must not be spreading but ascending to God by being burned.

We cannot and should not offer to God the burnt offering which He desires in the place of our choosing. We must leave our place and go to the place of God's choice. Ishmael, the archer, the bowman, went southward toward Egypt and married an Egyptian woman. But Isaac, the burnt offering, was a different kind of person. He did not go downward to Egypt; he went upward to Moriah. If you consult a map, you will see that Moriah is north from Beer-sheba. Here we have a picture of two types of persons—an archer and a burnt offering. Which will you be? (*Life-study of Genesis,* pp. 760, 758-759)

Further Reading: Life-study of Genesis, msg. 57; *Life-study of Romans,* msg. 8; *CWWN,* vol. 35, "The God of Abraham, Isaac, and Jacob," ch. 6

Enlightenment and inspiration: _____

_____

_____

_____

Morning Nourishment

Heb. **By faith Abraham, being tested, offered up Isaac;**
11:17 **indeed he who gladly received the promises was**
offering up his only begotten.
Rom. **Because out from Him and through Him and to Him**
11:36 **are all things. To Him be the glory forever. Amen.**

God told Abraham to offer Isaac, his only son whom he loved. How hard it must have been for Abraham to do this! If we had been he, we would have said, "Lord, I am more than a hundred twenty years of age, and Sarah is about to die. How can You ask me to offer back to You what You have given me?" If you have not had this experience, you will have it some day. We can testify that quite a number of times in the past God asked us to give back to Him what He had given us. The gifts, power, work, and success which He gives us must be offered back to Him. This is a real test. It would have been easy for Abraham to give up Lot or Eliezer. Even casting out Ishmael was not that difficult. But for him to offer his only son whom he loved was a very difficult thing. One day, after our having a good enjoyment of the Lord, He will ask us to give back to Him the gift, work, or success He has given us. He may say, "Now is the time for Me to ask you for something. I don't ask you to work for Me or to go to the mission field. I ask you to offer back what I have given you." This is the way we all must take today. (*Life-study of Genesis*, p. 757)

Today's Reading

Often after we have had the best enjoyment of the Lord, He will not ask us to do something for Him; rather, He will tell us to offer back to Him what He has given us. At such a time the Lord may say, "You have received a gift from and of Me. Now I ask you to return it." We always expect that after having a good time with the Lord He will command us to do something for Him. We never imagine that He may ask us to give back to Him that which He has given us. As Abraham was enjoying intimate fellowship with God, he was not commanded to work for Him. He received the highest demand from God—to give back to God what God had given him. From the very beginning, God never accepted anything that Abraham had. He did not care for Lot, rejected Eliezer, and told him to cast out Ishmael. Now, after Eliezer, Lot, and Ishmael had all been rejected, Abraham had acquired Isaac, the seed promised by God, and was at peace. Everything concerning Isaac was of God and by God. Never again would God say no to what Abraham had. But suddenly God came in and seemed to say, "I would never refuse Isaac. He was born of and from Me. But, Abraham, now you must give him back to Me."

Abraham was marvelous. If I had been he, I would have said, "Lord, what are You doing? You did not care for Lot, and You have refused Eliezer and Ishmael. Now You want Isaac, the one who was of You, to be given back to You. Will You rob me to such an extent?" If I had been Abraham, I would not have offered Isaac. I would have shook my head and said, "No, this certainly is not of the Lord. It would have been logical for Him to want Eliezer, and reasonable to demand Ishmael. But how could God want me to give Isaac back to Him? God is not purposeless. He promised to give me a seed, and His promise has been confirmed and fulfilled. Why would He now waste all that He has been doing with me?" Yes, God is a God of purpose, and He certainly had a purpose in asking Abraham to give Isaac back to Him.

Many Christians, including some Christian workers, have never learned the lesson of offering back to God what He has given them. Have you received a gift? Do not hold on to it. Sooner or later God will come in and say, "Offer back to Me the gift which I have given you." Has God given you a successful work? At a certain time, God may say, "This work is the Isaac which I have given to you. Now I want you to offer it back to Me."...All that God has given us, even what He has wrought in and through us, must be offered back to Him. (*Life-study of Genesis,* pp. 756-757)

Further Reading: Life-study of Genesis, msg. 57; *CWWN,* vol. 35, "The God of Abraham, Isaac, and Jacob," ch. 6

Enlightenment and inspiration: _____

_____

_____

_____

Morning Nourishment

Gen. And Abraham called the name of that place Jeho-
22:14 vah-jireh, as it is said *to* this day, On the mount of
Jehovah it will be provided.

Rev. And I saw, and behold, the Lamb standing on
14:1 Mount Zion, and with Him a hundred and forty-
four thousand, having His name and the name of
His Father written on their foreheads.

Praise the Lord that today we are Isaacs, not Ishmaels. We
are not journeying southward toward Egypt; we are traveling
northward to Mount Zion.

In order to see this, we must have the life at Beer-sheba,
because only this life builds us up and qualifies us to be the
burnt offering for God's satisfaction and to receive the vision.
The name Moriah means "the vision of Jah," that is, the vision
of Jehovah, the vision of the Lord. This has two meanings—
that we see the Lord and that the Lord sees us. On Mount
Moriah Abraham undoubtedly saw God and God saw him.
Likewise, on today's Mount Zion we have a vision. There is no
cloud here. We are not in darkness; we are in the vision. The
church life is a vision in which we see God and God sees us.
(*Life-study of Genesis,* pp. 764-765)

Today's Reading

The translators are troubled about how to render Genesis
22:14, uncertain whether it should be "in the mount of the Lord
it shall be seen" or "it shall be provided." According to the King
James Version, verse 14 says, "And Abraham called the name of
that place Jehovah-jireh: as it is said to this day, In the mount
of the Lord it shall be seen." Other versions say, "In the
mount of the Lord it shall be provided."…Although this verse is
difficult to translate, it is easy to understand according to our
experience. God's provision is always His vision. Whenever we
participate in and enjoy God's provision, we have a vision. We
see God and He sees us. Because we are in His provision and have
the vision, everything is clear, nothing is opaque, and there is

no separation between us and Him.

Where is God's provision today? It is in the church life on Mount Zion. We all can testify what a provision there is in the church life. As we are enjoying the provision, what a vision we have! We see God. We see eternity. Here in the church life everything is crystal clear and transparent in God's eyes and in ours, and nothing is opaque. We did not have this experience in Christianity. When we were there, we were in a low dungeon that was opaque on every side. But today in the church life on Mount Zion we have the full provision with the full vision. We see God and are seen by Him; God sees us and is seen by us. In God's provision, everything is transparent.

Abraham went to a primitive region, built an altar on a mountain, and there offered his only son Isaac (vv. 9-10). To build an altar there was not easy, and to offer his only son by killing him was even more difficult. But he did this. He truly meant business with the Lord. We also must build an altar and offer what God demands. This surely will cost us something.

We have seen the record of Abraham's obedience by faith. The faith with which he was thoroughly infused by God gave him this obedience. It was this infused faith that brought him to Mount Moriah where he enjoyed God's provision and had a thoroughly transparent vision from God. At that time there was no one on earth nor in the whole universe who was as clear about divine things as Abraham was. There, on Mount Moriah, Abraham experienced God's provision and received a clear vision. Everything was clear in his eyes. We must not read Genesis 22 merely as a story. We must receive divine light from it and see that Abraham's experience is being repeated in us today. Praise the Lord that we have today's Beer-sheba and Moriah. We are not going downward to Egypt; we are traveling upward to Mount Moriah, where we shall enjoy God's provision and have a transparent vision. (*Life-study of Genesis*, pp. 765-766)

Further Reading: Life-study of Genesis, msg. 57

Enlightenment and inspiration: _____

_____

_____

_____

Morning Nourishment

Heb. Counting that God was able to raise *men* even from
11:19 the dead, from which he also received him back in
figure.

Rom. ...In the sight of God whom he believed, who gives
4:17 life to the dead and calls the things not being as
being.

After Isaac was offered, he was returned in resurrection for the
fulfillment of God's eternal purpose (Gen. 22:4, 12-13, 16, 18).
After being returned in resurrection, Isaac was another person.
He was no longer the natural Isaac but the resurrected Isaac.
This is very encouraging. After we have offered to God what we
have received of Him, He will then return it to us in resurrection.
Every gift, spiritual blessing, work, and success we have received
of God must undergo the test of death. Eventually, it will come
back to us in resurrection. The Lord Jesus said, "Truly, truly, I say
to you, Unless the grain of wheat falls into the ground and dies, it
abides alone; but if it dies, it bears much fruit" (John 12:24). Suppose God gives you a certain natural gift. That is one grain of
wheat. If you keep this natural gift, never offering it to God, it will
remain as one grain. But if you offer it back to God, after it has
passed through death, it will be returned to you in resurrection
and become a blessing. It does not depend on what we can do or
intend to do for God. It all depends on our growing up to be offered
to God as a burnt offering and then being raised up from the dead
to be a resurrected gift....For one grain to be multiplied into a
hundred grains is God's blessing. If you offer your one grain to
God and allow Him to put it into death, it will be returned to you
in resurrection. Then you will see multiplication and great blessing. This is God's way. (*Life-study of Genesis*, pp. 761-762)

Today's Reading

In the Old Testament we cannot see why Abraham obeyed
God so quickly and boldly. But in the New Testament we see that
Abraham believed in the resurrecting God (Heb. 11:17-19; James
2:21-22). He had the faith which counted on God to raise up the

very Isaac whom he was about to slay. He had received the firm and even confirmed promise that God's covenant would be established with Isaac and that he would become a great nation (Gen. 17:19-21). If Abraham had offered Isaac on the altar, slaying him and burning him as an offering to God, and God did not raise him from the dead, then God's word would have been in vain. Abraham's faith was based upon God's confirmed promise. Abraham could have said, "If God wants Isaac, I will just slay him. God will raise him up for the fulfillment of His promise."

[In Romans 4:17] we see that Abraham believed in God for two things: for giving life to the dead and for calling things not being as being. The birth of Isaac was related to God's calling things not being as being, and his being returned was related to God's giving life to the dead. Because Abraham had such faith, he obeyed God's commandment immediately. Hebrews 11:17-19 says that when Abraham was tried, he offered up Isaac by faith, "counting that God was able to raise men even from the dead, from which he also received him back in figure." (*Life-study of Genesis*, pp. 762-763)

Before the Lord, we have to realize that even the commission we have received, the work we are doing, and the will of God that we know, must be dropped. There is a big difference between what is natural and what is of resurrection. Everything that we do not want to let go of is natural. Everything that comes from resurrection is preserved by God, and we cannot hold on to it with our fleshly hands. We have to learn to thank the Lord for calling us to His work and also learn to thank Him for calling us to not work. We are not directly related to God's work but to God Himself....What is resurrection? Resurrection is anything that we cannot put our hands on, that we cannot hold on to. This is resurrection. Natural things are the things that we can grasp hold of, while we cannot grasp hold of the things in resurrection. (*CWWN*, vol. 35, "The God of Abraham, Isaac, and Jacob," p. 84)

Further Reading: Life-study of Genesis, msg. 57; *CWWN,* vol. 35, ch. 6; *The God of Resurrection*

Enlightenment and inspiration: _____

_____

_____

_____

Morning Nourishment

Gen. ...Because you have done this thing and
22:16-18 have not withheld your son, your only son, I
will surely bless you and will greatly multiply your seed like the stars of the heavens
and like the sand which is on the seashore;
and your seed shall possess the gate of his
enemies. And in your seed all the nations of
the earth shall be blessed...

Abraham was blessed with two categories of people, one likened to the stars of the heaven (Gen. 22:17; 15:5) and the other
to the sand upon the seashore (22:17), which is also likened to
the dust of the earth (13:16)....We, the Christians, are the stars,
the heavenly descendants of Abraham; and the genuine Jews,
God's earthly people, are the sand, the dust. Eventually, the
Jewish people will be God's priests on earth and will teach all
the nations. This is prophesied clearly in Zechariah 8:20-23.
Why are the Jews described both as the sand and as the dust?
The sea signifies the world corrupted by Satan, and the dust is
of the earth created by God. The Jews have been restored to
God's creation. Hence, they are signified by the sand which is
the dust beside the sea. Although they are an earthly people,
they are not the dust under the sea but the dust, the sand,
by the seashore. They are separated from the corrupted sea,
Satan's corrupted world. However, the stars are not only separated from the corrupted world but are also heavenly. (*Life-
study of Genesis,* pp. 772-773)

Today's Reading

The star is sown as a seed in Genesis 22 and will be harvested
in Revelation 20 and 21. The New Jerusalem is composed of the
twelve tribes of Israel, representing the Old Testament saints,
and the twelve apostles, representing the New Testament believers. Those represented by the apostles are the heavenly
stars, and those represented by the twelve tribes are the sand of
the seashore. These two peoples eventually will be built together

into the eternal New Jerusalem. Hence, the eternal New Jerusalem will be the ultimate consummation of Abraham's seed. This is God's blessing to Abraham.

After seeing this, we need to say, "Praise the Lord, God's blessing is not a good house, car, degree, promotion, wife, or child. It is the multiplication of the saints in God's recovery and the multiplication of the churches." I hope that one day a part of the New Jerusalem will be our multiplication as God's blessing to us. At that time, all the cars and houses will be gone. Only the multiplication in God's blessing will remain forever. We shall see the blessing in God's multiplication in the New Jerusalem for eternity.

Here in Genesis 22 we see a basic principle, that is, whatever God gives us will be multiplied. God gave Abraham one Isaac, and Abraham offered him back to God. Then this one Isaac was multiplied into numberless stars and sand. If Abraham would not have offered Isaac back to God, he might have had only one Isaac. But having been offered back to God by Abraham, Isaac was multiplied into the New Jerusalem. This is the way to have God's gift multiplied in us—offer back to God what He has given us.

Ultimately, all the heavenly stars and the earthly sand will be in Christ. As we have pointed out in the past, the New Jerusalem will be a great, corporate Christ. In the four Gospels we have the individual Christ, but at the end of Revelation we have the corporate Christ including all true believers.

In this one seed, Christ, all the nations of the earth shall be blessed. Have not the United States, Germany, Japan, China, and Great Britain been blessed? This is God's blessing. May we all expect that the blessing which we shall receive of God will be the multiplication that will issue in Christ, the unique seed. The multiplication that will spread to Europe, Africa, and throughout the earth must simply be Christ. All the churches on earth will just be the multiplication of Christ. (*Life-study of Genesis,* pp. 773-774)

Further Reading: Life-study of Genesis, msg. 58

Enlightenment and inspiration: _____

_____

_____

_____

Morning Nourishment

Heb. **But you have come forward to Mount Zion**
12:22-23 **and to the city of the living God, the heav-**
enly Jerusalem; and to myriads of angels, to
the universal gathering; and to the church
of the firstborn, who have been enrolled in
the heavens; and to God, the Judge of all;
and to the spirits of righteous men who
have been made perfect.

Abraham went to Mount Moriah, the place of God's choice. In Genesis 22:2 God told Abraham to go into the land of Moriah and offer Isaac on one of the mountains of which He would tell him. In the next verse we are told that Abraham "rose up and went to the place of which God had told him." Before Abraham began his journey, God must have told him which mountain He had chosen. In verse 4 we are told that "on the third day Abraham lifted up his eyes and saw the place from afar." Abraham did nothing according to his concept or choice; he did everything according to God's revelation. (*Life-study of Genesis*, p. 763)

Today's Reading

What Abraham did in Genesis 22 is an important seed in the Bible. As I have already pointed out, Abraham's descendants, the children of Israel, were commanded by God to go three times a year to Mount Moriah to worship God and there to offer to Him their burnt offerings. We have seen that Mount Moriah became Mount Zion, the very center of the good land. Abraham was the first to worship God with the burnt offering on Mount Zion. Eventually, we all shall be on Mount Zion worshipping God. On the one hand, in the church life today, as true descendants of Abraham, we are on Mount Zion; on the other hand, we are on our way there. What Abraham did in chapter twenty-two was the seed. His descendants, the Israelites, were the development of this seed, and we today are the further development of the seed. We all, including Abraham, shall be in the harvest of the seed. Perhaps one day we shall shake hands with Abraham on the eternal Mount Zion and say to him, "You were on the ancient Mount Zion, we were on the new testament Mount Zion, and now we are all together here on the eternal Mount Zion." (*Life-study of Genesis,* pp. 763-764)

Jerusalem is built on the top of a mountain. Although Jerusalem is good, it is not the peak. In Jerusalem there is a peak, that is, Mount Zion, on which the temple was built. About one thousand years before the building of the temple, God asked Abraham to offer his son Isaac on Mount Moriah, which is another name for Mount Zion (Gen. 22:2; 2 Chron. 3:1). The good situation in the recovery today is just like Jerusalem. However, there is no Zion. In the New Testament the overcomers are likened to Zion. In Revelation 14:1 the 144,000 overcomers are not just in Jerusalem; they are on the peak of Zion. The overcomers, the vital groups, are today's Zion. My burden today is to help you reach the peak of the vital groups, that is, the overcomers' Zion. Although we may have a good church life, among us there is almost no realization, no practicality, no actuality, and no reality of the Body life. This is the need in the recovery today.

There is no other way to reach this high peak except by praying. It is more than evident that Jerusalem is here as a big realm of Christians, but where is Zion, the overcomers? In the book of Revelation what the Lord wants and what the Lord will build up is Zion, the overcomers. The overcomers are the very Zion, where God is. This is the intrinsic reality of the spiritual revelation in the holy Word of God. We have to realize what the Lord's recovery is. The Lord's recovery is to build up Zion. Paul's writings unveil this to the uttermost, but not many saw this in the past. (*The Practical Points concerning Blending,* pp. 16-17, 46-47).

Further Reading: Life-study of Genesis, msg. 58; *The Practical Points concerning Blending,* chs. 2-5*

Enlightenment and inspiration: _____
_____
_____
_____

Hymns, #403

1 Live Thyself, Lord Jesus, through me,
      For my very life art Thou;
   Thee I take to all my problems
      As the full solution now.
   Live Thyself, Lord Jesus, through me,
      In all things Thy will be done;
   I but a transparent vessel
      To make visible the Son.

2 Consecrated is Thy temple,
      Purged from every stain and sin;
   May Thy flame of glory now be
      Manifested from within.
   Let the earth in solemn wonder
      See my body willingly
   Offered as Thy slave obedient,
      Energized alone by Thee.

3 Every moment, every member,
      Girded, waiting Thy command;
   Underneath the yoke to labor
      Or be laid aside as planned.
   When restricted in pursuing,
      No disquiet will beset;
   Underneath Thy faithful dealing
      Not a murmur or regret.

4 Ever tender, quiet, restful,
      Inclinations put away,
   That Thou may for me choose freely
      As Thy finger points the way.
   Live Thyself, Lord Jesus, through me,
      For my very life art Thou;
   Thee I take to all my problems
      As the full solution now.

Composition for prophecy with main point and sub-points: _____

_____

_____

_____

_____

_____

_____

_____

_____

_____

_____

_____

_____

_____

_____

_____

_____

_____

_____

_____

_____

_____

_____

_____

_____

_____

_____

_____

_____

_____

_____

_____

_____

_____

_____

A Practical Living
in Oneness with the Lord
and a Type of Christ Marrying the Church

Scripture Reading: Gen. 24; Eph. 3:8-11; 5:25-27

Day 1 I. **The primary point in Genesis 24 is the practical living in oneness with the Lord for the fulfilling of God's purpose:**

A. Abraham's living was a practical living in oneness with the Lord:

1. Although there is no record of God telling Abraham to take a wife for his son from his own country, Abraham had this understanding; it came from his living in accordance with God's concept; because Abraham lived in oneness with God, he knew God's will and mind and acted in accordance with God's inner feeling (vv. 1-6, 40; cf. 1 Cor. 7:25; 2 Cor. 2:10; Phil. 1:8).

2. Abraham was a man who lived in oneness with God (James 2:23; 2 Chron. 20:7; Isa. 41:8); if we love the Lord and live in oneness with Him, whatever we say and do will be in accordance with His likes and dislikes and with His inner will and His mind.

3. If we live in oneness with the Lord, He will not need to tell us what He desires, because we shall already know His inner feeling by being one with Him; we need such a living for the fulfillment of God's purpose today.

4. Abraham moved in accordance with God's economy; what he did in obtaining a wife for Isaac was for the fulfillment of God's eternal purpose (Gen. 24:3-8).

5. The primary thing revealed in Genesis 24 is the practical living in accordance with God's economy for the carrying out of His eternal purpose; we need a life resembling

that of Abraham; his motive, his action, and everything he did were in accordance with God's economy (Rom. 4:12; cf. 1 Sam. 4:3, footnote 1).

Day 2

6. Genesis 24:40 indicates that Abraham walked before the Lord; since he walked in the Lord's presence, whatever he did was God's will and according to His economy.

7. Abraham did not charge his servant to be faithful, to be honest, or to do a good work; he charged him with and by the Lord (vv. 2-3, 9, 40-41); by charging his servant with the Lord, he brought him deep into the Lord.

B. Abraham's oldest servant was faithful in responsibility (vv. 5, 9, 33, 54, 56):

1. Abraham's servant followed in Abraham's footsteps by trusting in the Lord for his responsibility; he prayed to the Lord in a clear, humble, yet simple way; everyone who truly believes in God is simple (vv. 12-14, 21, 42; cf. 2 Cor. 1:12; 11:2-3).

2. The servant knew the Lord's will by looking for His leading and sovereignty in the environment (Gen. 24:13-21, 26-27, 48-49).

Day 3

C. Rebekah was chaste, kind, and diligent (vv. 16, 18-20); she was also absolute in her decision to take Isaac as her husband (vv. 57-58, 61) and was submissive to Isaac (vv. 64-65); as such, she is an excellent type of the church as the bride, the wife, of Christ (cf. Eph. 5:23-25).

D. Laban and Bethuel were in the fear of the Lord; they were also very hospitable (Gen. 24:31-33, 50-51, 55-60).

E. Isaac was meditating in the field to seek the Lord; after the servant told Isaac all that had happened, Isaac took what his father had done for him and married Rebekah; his marriage eventually fulfilled the purpose of God (vv. 63, 66-67; 21:12b; 22:17-18).

F. The life of those in Genesis 24 was not merely for their own human living; it was a life that issued in the fulfillment of God's eternal purpose, a life that brought forth Christ and produced the kingdom of God for God's economy; thus, in the gaining of a wife for Isaac, everything was done according to God's economy to bring forth Christ for the producing of the kingdom of God (v. 40; 22:17-18; Gal. 3:16, 29).

Day 4 II. **In Genesis 24 there is an account of the marriage of Isaac with four main persons: Abraham typifies God the Father, Isaac typifies God the Son, the servant typifies God the Spirit, and Rebekah typifies the chosen people of God, who will marry the Son and become His counterpart (John 3:29; 2 Cor. 11:2; Eph. 5:25-32; Rev. 19:7-9; 21:2, 9-10):**

A. In eternity past God the Father had an eternal purpose, an eternal plan, to gain the church as a bride for His Son out of the human race (Eph. 3:8-11; 2:10; Matt. 9:15):

1. Abraham, a type of the Father, charged his servant, a type of the Holy Spirit, not to take a wife for his son from the daughters of the Canaanites but from Abraham's relatives (Gen. 24:3-4, 7).

2. In typology the fact that Isaac's bride was taken from Abraham's relatives indicates that the counterpart of Christ must come from Christ's race, not from the angels or from any other creatures; since Christ was incarnated to be a man, humanity has become His race (cf. 2:21-22; 1:26; Acts 17:28-29a; John 1:14; Rev. 22:17a).

Day 5 B. In time God the Father commissioned God the Spirit, sent Him on an errand, to carry out the Father's plan by going to reach and contact the chosen bride and bring her to God the Son to be His counterpart, His wife (Gen. 24:3):

1. Just as the servant was hunting for a wife for Isaac, the Spirit is hunting for a wife for God the Son through His seeking sanctification (vv. 11-14, 24; John 4:6-7, 10; 1 Pet. 1:2; Luke 15:8-10; John 16:8-11).

Day 6

2. Just as the servant brought the riches of Isaac to Rebekah, the Spirit brings the riches of Christ to the bride (Gen. 24:10, 22, 47, 53; John 16:13-15):

   a. After the camels had finished drinking, the servant put a golden nose-ring upon Rebekah's nose and two bracelets upon her hands (Gen. 24:22, 47):

      (1) The putting of the nose-ring, weighing half a shekel, upon Rebekah's nose signifies that her "smelling" function had been caught by the divine nature with the foretaste of the Spirit, which guarantees that the full taste is coming (cf. S. S. 7:4, 8; 2:3; Heb. 6:4-6; Lev. 21:18; 1 Cor. 2:15; Rom. 8:23; Eph. 1:13-14).

      (2) The putting of the bracelets, weighing ten gold shekels, upon Rebekah's hands signifies that we are "handcuffed" by the Spirit to receive the complete divine function for the service in the Body of Christ (1 Tim. 2:8; Eph. 3:1; 4:1; 6:20; Rom. 12:4; 1 Cor. 12:4-11; Matt. 25:15).

   b. Rebekah also received silver jewelry, gold jewelry, and clothing (Gen. 24:53), all of which indicate that in the church life all the riches of Christ are ours:

      (1) Just as the servant imparted Isaac's wealth to Rebekah for her beautification in order for her to return to Isaac for his glorification, the Spirit transmits the riches of Christ's glory

into us for our beautification so that we may return to Christ as His bride for His glorification (vv. 47, 53, 61-67; Eph. 3:16, 21).

(2) We are adorned to be Christ's bride by the dispensing of His unsearchable riches into us through the Spirit's dispositional sanctification (Rev. 21:2, 19a; Isa. 54:10-13; 1 Thes. 5:23; Eph. 3:8):

(a) To receive the dispensing of Christ in His unsearchable riches, we must know, we must use, and we must exercise our spirit, caring for the sanctifying Spirit's speaking and working in our spirit (Rom. 15:16; Eph. 1:17; 2:22; 3:5, 16; 4:23; 5:18; 6:18).

(b) To receive the dispensing of Christ in His unsearchable riches, we must be sanctified by the metabolic cleansing of the instant, present, and living word of Christ (5:26-27; cf. S. S. 8:13-14; Rev. 1:20).

3. Just as Rebekah was convinced by the servant to marry Isaac, the Spirit attracts us to Christ and causes us to love Him whom we have not seen (Gen. 24:54-58; 1 Pet. 1:8; 2:7; cf. *Hymns,* #546):

a. The Spirit comes to the believers and testifies to them of the riches of Christ, which He has received from the Father (cf. Gen. 24:35-36), causing the believers to be attracted to Christ and to love Him, to forsake the world, and to leave their natural relations in the flesh (v. 58) to be joined to Christ (Matt. 19:29), even though they have never seen Him (1 Pet. 1:8).

b. Before Rebekah met Isaac in the good land, she had participated in and enjoyed Isaac's inheritance through the servant's gifts; likewise, before we meet Christ, we enjoy the gifts of the Spirit as a foretaste of the full taste of His riches (Gen. 24:53; Heb. 6:4; Rom. 8:23).

4. Just as the servant brought Rebekah to Isaac, the Spirit is bringing us to Christ to present us to Christ as His lovely bride (Gen. 24:51, 58, 61-67; 2 Cor. 1:21-22; 3:6, 8, 17-18; 13:14).

C. Isaac received Rebekah in the evening, signifying that the marriage of Christ will be at the evening, the close, of this age (Gen. 24:63-64):

1. Isaac brought Rebekah into the tent of Sarah, his mother, and loved Rebekah, signifying that Christ will receive His bride in grace as well as in love (v. 67; 1 Tim. 1:14; Eph. 6:24; Rev. 22:21).

2. After marrying Rebekah, Isaac was comforted, satisfied; likewise, Christ will be satisfied on the day of His marriage; our comfort is His comfort, and His satisfaction is our satisfaction (19:7; cf. 2 Cor. 5:9; Heb. 11:5-6).

Morning Nourishment

Gen. **...You will not take a wife for my son from the**
24:3-4 **daughters of the Canaanites, among whom I am**
dwelling. But you shall go to my country and to my
relatives, and take a wife for my son Isaac.
22:17 **I will surely bless you and will greatly multiply**
your seed like the stars of the heavens and like the
sand which is on the seashore; and your seed shall
possess the gate of his enemies.

According to the common understanding of most Christians, the main point of Genesis 24 is that Isaac is a type of Christ as the Bridegroom and that Rebekah is a type of the church as the bride. However, this is not the main point. The primary point is the practical living in oneness with the Lord for the fulfilling of God's purpose....We must forget all we have learned in the past and look to the Lord for something new.

What then is the purpose of the marriage in Genesis 24? Is it simply that a single man might have a happy, comfortable life? No. If you consider the Bible as a whole, you will see that Isaac's marriage was altogether for the fulfillment of God's eternal purpose....If this single man was to have seed for the fulfillment of God's eternal purpose, he had to get married....God [had] said [to Abraham], "I will surely bless you and will greatly multiply your seed like the stars of the heavens and like the sand which is on the seashore; and your seed shall possess the gate of his enemies. And in your seed all the nations of the earth shall be blessed" (22:17-18). Here we also have the seed for the fulfillment of God's purpose. Thus, Isaac's marriage was not common nor merely for his human living; it was for the fulfillment of God's eternal purpose. (*Life-study of Genesis,* pp. 788-790)

Today's Reading

Abraham's living was a practical living in oneness with the Lord. Abraham did not suddenly have a vision in which God told him that He had a high purpose to carry out on earth, that He needed him, and that Isaac had to be married in order for God's purpose to be fulfilled....There is no record that God said, "Abraham, let Me charge you to send someone to your own country to get a wife for Isaac. I will never allow you to take a Canaanite woman as a wife for your son." Although there is no record of God's saying this, Abraham did have this understanding.

Although Abraham was desperate to take care of his son's marriage, he would not accept a Canaanite as Isaac's wife.... [Abraham] sent his oldest servant far away, back to the country from where he came, to find a wife for Isaac. Although God never told Abraham to do this, what Abraham did was according to 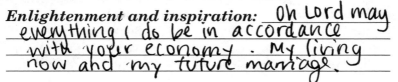 God's inner will and concept....When we live in oneness with Him, we shall share His concept, and whatever we think and do will be in accordance with His feeling. God will not need to say anything, for we shall sense what He senses, knowing His inner feeling because we live in oneness with Him.

Abraham moved in accordance with God's economy (Gen. 24:3-8). What he did in obtaining a wife for Isaac was for the fulfillment of God's eternal purpose. We long to see that all the marriages in the churches will be for the fulfillment of God's purpose. This kind of marriage requires a daily living in oneness with God. Young brothers, if everything you do is in accordance with God's economy, even your marriage will be the carrying out of His economy. You need to say, "Lord, what I am doing here today must be in accordance with Your economy. I am single now, but one day I will be married. May my marriage be for Your economy." This is the main revelation in Genesis 24. The primary thing in this chapter is not that Isaac is a type of Christ as the Bridegroom and that Rebekah is a type of the church as the bride. I say again that the primary thing revealed here is the practical living in accordance with God's economy for the carrying out of His eternal purpose. We need a life which resembles that of Abraham. His motive, action, and everything he did were in accordance with God's economy. (*Life-study of Genesis,* pp. 790-792)

Further Reading: Life-study of Genesis, msg. 60

Enlightenment and inspiration: Oh Lord may everything I do be in accordance with your economy. My living now and my future marriage.

Morning Nourishment

Gen. And he said to me, Jehovah, before whom I walk,
24:40 will send His angel with you and make your journey prosperous. And you shall take a wife for my
son from my family, even from my father's house.
48 And I bowed and worshipped Jehovah and blessed
Jehovah, the God of my master Abraham, who had
led me in the right way to take the daughter of my
master's brother for his son.

Abraham did not act in today's traditional, religious way, fasting and praying to seek the Lord's will. He did not suddenly have a dream in which he saw Rebekah in the land of Chaldea waiting for Abraham's servant. As Genesis 24:40 indicates, Abraham walked before the Lord. As a person walking in the presence of the Lord, he did not need to fast or pray in order to know God's will. Since he walked in the Lord's presence, whatever he did was God's will and according to God's economy. (*Life-study of Genesis*, pp. 792-793)

Today's Reading

Abraham did not charge his servant to be faithful, honest, or to do a good work; he charged him with and by the Lord (Gen. 24:2-3, 9, 40-41). Here we see that the atmosphere in which Abraham lived was the Lord Himself. By charging his servant with the Lord, he brought him deep into the Lord. Likewise, we should not charge people with our wisdom or even with our love, but with the Lord.

Abraham believed in the sovereign Lord, telling his servant that the Lord would send His angel with him and prosper his way (v. 40). Abraham seemed to be saying, "God will send His angel before you. Although I am sending you to do the job, I believe in God. In a sense, I don't believe that you can accomplish this work, but I trust in the living God. You don't need to be burdened or to worry. Just go and do the job, for my God will send His angel to do the work for you." What a life Abraham had!...[Abraham] only charged his servant to serve by the

Lord, assuring him that God would send His angel before him and prosper his way. Here we see Abraham's living faith.

Abraham's oldest servant was faithful in responsibility (vv. 5, 9, 33, 54, 56). He followed Abraham's footsteps in being faithful. I believe that he was infused by and with Abraham's life, seeing how Abraham did everything by trusting in the Lord. As a result, the servant also trusted in Him.

Abraham's servant trusted in the Lord for his responsibility (vv. 12, 21, 42). He prayed to the Lord in a clear, humble, yet simple way. Everyone who truly believes in God is simple. When he came to the well near the city of Nahor, he prayed, saying, "O Jehovah, the God of my master Abraham, please grant me success today, and show lovingkindness to my master Abraham. I am standing here by the spring of water as the daughters of the men of the city are coming out to draw water. And may it be that the girl to whom I say, Please let down your pitcher that I may drink, and who says, Drink, and I will also give your camels a drink, may she be the one whom You have appointed for Your servant, for Isaac; and in this I will know that You have shown kindness to my master" (vv. 12-14). His prayer was answered immediately. Before he had even finished speaking, Rebekah came with her pitcher upon her shoulder. When he asked her for a drink, she not only gave him a drink but also drew water for all his camels. After she had done this, the servant was clear that Rebekah was the one and he gave her a ring and two bracelets.

The servant knew the Lord's will by looking for His leading in the environment (vv. 13-21, 26-27, 48-49). We also can see God's sovereignty in our environment. No one told the servant to go to the city of Nahor, the city of Abraham's brother. He just went there, and at the well he met Rebekah, Nahor's granddaughter. Nothing was accidental; everything was ordained before the foundation of the world and was carried out through Abraham's servant, a man who trusted in God. (*Life-study of Genesis*, pp. 793-794)

Further Reading: Life-study of Genesis, msg. 60

Enlightenment and inspiration: _____

_____

_____

_____

Morning Nourishment

Gen. **And the girl was very beautiful in appearance, a vir-**
24:16 **gin, and no man had known her. And she went down**
to the spring and filled her pitcher and came up.
  20 **And she hurried and emptied her pitcher into the**
trough and ran again to the well to draw *water,*
and she drew *it* **for all his camels.**

Rebekah was chaste and pure. She was also kind and diligent
(Gen. 24:18-20). When Abraham's servant asked for a drink, she
immediately gave it to him. She also drew water for his camels. It
was hard work for a young woman to draw water out of the well
and pour it into the trough for ten camels to drink, but she did it. If
the young sisters want to be under God's sovereignty, especially
with respect to their marriage, they need to be kind and diligent.
Any young woman who is unkind and sloppy should remain single. When people ask you to do one thing, you must do two things
for them. And the second thing should far surpass the first thing.
You should not only give a man water to drink, but should also
draw water for his ten camels. If you do this, you will be qualified
to obtain your husband, your Isaac. This is some advice to all the
young single sisters. (*Life-study of Genesis,* pp. 794-795)

Today's Reading

Rebekah was absolute (Gen. 24:57-58, 61). Although Rebekah
had never seen Isaac, she was willing to go to him without hesi-
tation. She did not say to her mother, "Mother, I have never seen
Isaac. Perhaps I should correspond with him first and after-
ward have him pay us a visit. Then I could decide whether or
not to marry him." Rebekah did not talk in this way. Although
her brother and mother were hesitating, wanting her to stay
for at least ten days, she said, "I will go." She was absolute.

Rebekah was also submissive (vv. 64-65). When she saw
Isaac and realized who he was, "she took her veil and covered
herself." Sisters, do not put a piece of cloth on your head as a
decoration or ornament. It must be a sign of your submission.
Once you are married, you are no longer your own head. Your

husband is your head, and your head must be covered. This is the true meaning of marriage.

Laban and Bethuel were in the fear of the Lord (vv. 29-31). They were also very hospitable (vv. 31-33). Hospitality often brings in the greatest blessing. For Rebekah, the daughter of Bethuel and the sister of Laban, to become Isaac's wife was a great blessing. That blessing was secured by their being hospitable. If they had not been hospitable but rather had rejected Abraham's servant, that wonderful marriage would never have taken place. Furthermore, they accepted the Lord's sovereignty, saying, "The matter comes from Jehovah; we cannot speak to you bad or good" (vv. 50-51, 55-60). Laban and Bethuel recognized that this was the Lord's doing and that they had no right to say anything about it. Here we see the atmosphere of their life, a life in oneness with God.

Isaac was not a man of activity, for he did not do anything. He simply dwelt by a well, by a place of living water. Verse 63 says, "And Isaac went out to meditate in the field toward evening."...He went out to the field to seek the Lord and meditate before God. While he was meditating, Rebekah came. After the servant had told Isaac all that had happened, Isaac took what his father had done for him and married Rebekah (vv. 66-67). His marriage was an inheritance, not a strife....He did not do a thing to get a wife. He only took what the father had secured for him. Acting in this way, he was one with the Lord that the purpose of God might be fulfilled in him. He had a real and solid marriage without a wedding ceremony.

Isaac's marriage eventually fulfilled the purpose of God (21:12b; 22:17-18). The life of those in chapter 24 was not merely for their own human living; it was a life that issued in the fulfillment of God's eternal purpose, a life which brought forth Christ and produced the kingdom of God for God's economy. (*Life-study of Genesis,* pp. 795-797)

Further Reading: Life-study of Genesis, msg. 60

Enlightenment and inspiration: _____

_____

_____

_____

Morning Nourishment

Gen. And Abraham said to his servant, the oldest of his
24:2-4 house, who ruled over all that he had, Put your
hand under my thigh; and I will make you swear
by Jehovah, the God of heaven and the God of
earth, that you will not take a wife for my son from
the daughters of the Canaanites, among whom I
am dwelling. But you shall go to my country and to
my relatives, and take a wife for my son Isaac.

In this account of the marriage of Isaac, Abraham typifies
God the Father, the servant typifies God the Spirit, Isaac typifies God the Son, and Rebekah typifies the chosen people of God,
who will marry the Son and become His counterpart. The entire
New Testament is a record of the Triune God working together
to gain a part of the human race to be the bride, the counterpart,
of the Son (John 3:29; 2 Cor. 11:2; Eph. 5:25-32; Rev. 19:7-9; 21:2,
9-10). In eternity past God the Father had an eternal purpose
and made an eternal plan to gain the church as a bride for His
Son out of the human race (Eph. 3:8-11). Then, in time, God the
Father commissioned God the Spirit to carry out His plan by
going to contact the chosen bride and bring her to God the Son to
be His counterpart, His wife. (Gen. 24:2, footnote 2)

Today's Reading

In Genesis 24 we have four main persons: the father, the son,
the servant, and the bride. This is very meaningful. As we come
to the New Testament, we see that the Triune God is working
together to obtain a bride for the Son....The subject of the New
Testament is the Triune God, the Father, the Son, and the Spirit,
working together to obtain the bride for the Son. The Father
made the plan, the Spirit carries out the Father's plan, and the
Son enjoys what the Father has planned and what the Spirit
carries out. Who is the bride? The bride is a part of the human
race which will marry the Son and become His counterpart.
Matthew 28:19 speaks of the Father, the Son, and the Spirit. In
the Acts and Epistles we see how the Spirit works according to

the Father's plan to obtain the bride for the Son. At the end of the New Testament, in the book of Revelation, we see the bride. Revelation 19:7 says, "The marriage of the Lamb has come, and His wife has made herself ready." Ultimately, the whole New Jerusalem, a city-lady, will be the bride (Rev. 21:2, 9-10)....The New Jerusalem will be a female, the wife of the Lamb, the counterpart of the Son of God.

Firstly, we have the Father's plan....Ephesians 3:11 speaks of "the eternal purpose which He made in Christ Jesus our Lord."...When we speak of God's plan we are referring to God's purpose. In eternity past God made a plan, a plan to have the church for Christ (Eph. 3:8-11)....God's plan is to have a bride for His Son.

In the four Gospels the Lord Jesus told His disciples that He was the Bridegroom (Matt. 9:15). He came not only to save sinners but to have the bride....Christ came not merely to be our Savior and Redeemer; He also came to be the Bridegroom....God planned to take a part of the human race and make them the counterpart of His dear Son. Eventually, in the new heaven and the new earth, we shall not have a group of pitiful sinners; we shall have the bride, the New Jerusalem, the wife of the Lamb.

As we have seen, God the Father planned to take a bride for His Son out of the human race. Abraham, a type of the Father, charged his servant, a type of the Holy Spirit, not to take a wife for his son from the daughters of the Canaanites but from Abraham's kindred (Gen. 24:4, 7). In typology, this indicates that the counterpart of Christ must come from Christ's race, not from the angels nor from any other creatures. Since Christ was incarnated as a man, humanity has become His race....Because humanity is the race of Christ, it is dear and precious to God. Only out of humanity can God obtain the counterpart for His Son. (*Life-study of Genesis,* pp. 800-802)

Further Reading: The Issue of the Dispensing of the Processed Trinity and the Transmitting of the Transcending Christ, chs. 1-3

Enlightenment and inspiration: _____

_____

_____

_____

Morning Nourishment

Gen. 24:33 And *food* was set before him to eat. But he said, I will not eat until I have stated my business. And he said, Speak on.

1 Pet. 1:2 Chosen according to the foreknowledge of God the Father in the sanctification of the Spirit unto the obedience and sprinkling of the blood of Jesus Christ...

While the father had a plan, the servant received a commission, an errand (Gen. 24:33). Abraham commissioned him to go to his race and take a wife for his son. This signifies that God the Father has commissioned God the Spirit.

As Abraham commissioned his servant to reach the chosen bride (vv. 10-21), so God the Father commissioned God the Spirit to reach the human race. We all can testify that at a certain time the Spirit of God came to us. Perhaps you would say, "I didn't realize that God the Spirit came to me. I only know that someone preached the gospel to me." As that person was preaching the gospel to you, you were attracted by what he said and were willing to receive it. Although you did not understand everything he was saying, something deep within you was responding. In our mentality, many of us said, "I don't like this," but deep within our spirit we said, "This is very good." (*Life-study of Genesis*, pp. 802-803)

Today's Reading

Rebekah never dreamed that she would be selected to be Isaac's wife. According to the custom of the time, she simply went to draw water late in the afternoon. But on this day something special happened. Before she came to the well, Abraham's servant was already there. This indicates the Spirit's coming to the human race (Gen. 24:10). Before we ever heard the preaching of the gospel or came to a gospel meeting, the Holy Spirit was already there waiting.

In Genesis 24, Abraham's servant, who had come to a well (v. 11), asked a woman to give him a drink of water (v. 17). In John 4, the Lord Jesus, who had come to Jacob's well (John 4:6), also asked a woman for a drink. Preachers often say that we are thirsty and need the living water to quench our thirst. But have you ever heard that the Holy Spirit is thirsty and needs you to quench His thirst? In Genesis 24 we see a servant who was thirsty after his long journey, and in John 4 we see a Savior who was thirsty after His tiring journey. Who was more thirsty in Genesis 24, the servant or Rebekah? The servant was. Likewise, who was more thirsty in John 4, the Lord Jesus or the Samaritan woman?...Hence, as we preach the gospel, we must tell people that the Father, Son, and Spirit are thirsty for them.

As Rebekah went to draw water from the well that day, she was completely innocent, having no idea of what was to happen to her. She did not realize that by giving a man a drink of water and by drawing water for his camels she would be caught. But the father far away had made a plan to take a woman from her race as the wife for his son and had commissioned his servant to carry out this plan. Thus, the servant came to the city of Nahor and purposely waited there by the well. He was a real hunter hunting for a wife for Isaac. If Rebekah had never spoken to the servant, she would not have been caught. But, as we have seen, what happened did not depend on her. The servant had already prayed that the Lord would give him success....While he was still speaking in this way, Rebekah came. When he asked her for a drink of water, she not only gave him a drink, but said, "I will draw water for your camels also, until they have finished drinking" (Gen. 24:18-19). Although Rebekah did not realize it, in doing this, she was caught.

Abraham's servant eventually reached Rebekah through the satisfying water (v. 14). God's chosen ones are the satisfying water to the Holy Spirit. Today the Holy Spirit comes to seek God's chosen ones as Christ did at the well of Sychar (John 4:7). If anyone responds to Him and satisfies His desire, this is a sign that he is one of those chosen for Christ and that he will be gained by the Holy Spirit for Christ. (*Life-study of Genesis,* pp. 803-805)

Further Reading: The Spirit with Our Spirit, chs. 9, 11

Enlightenment and inspiration: _____

_____

_____

_____

Morning Nourishment

Gen. **And when the camels had finished drinking, the**
24:22 **man took a golden nose-ring weighing half a shekel**
and two bracelets for her hands weighing ten gold
shekels.

1 Pet. **Whom having not seen, you love; into whom though**
1:8 **not seeing** *Him* **at present, yet believing, you exult**
with joy *that is* **unspeakable and full of glory.**

The Spirit...brings the riches of Christ to the bride (Gen.
24:10, 22, 47, 53)....That Rebekah had a ring on her nose and
bracelets upon her hands meant that she had been caught. After
giving her these things, the servant asked her, "Whose daughter
are you? Please tell me, is there room in your father's house for us
to lodge in?" (v. 23). Once the servant was brought into Rebekah's
home, he testified of Isaac's riches. After Rebekah's brother Laban
and father Bethuel accepted the servant's proposal, he gave
Rebekah more of Isaac's riches, articles of silver, articles of gold,
and clothing (v. 53). He also gave precious things to her brother
and her mother. This is exactly what John 16:13-15 reveals concerning the Spirit. In these verses, the Lord Jesus said that the
Spirit will not speak of Himself, but that He will glorify the Son.
All that the Father has is His, and the Spirit receives of His and
discloses it to the disciples....The testimony of Abraham's servant
was not poor; rather, it was very rich. The servant said that the
Lord had blessed his master Abraham, that he had become great,
that he had given all things to his son Isaac, and that his master
had charged him to find a wife for his son. As Rebekah was listen-
ing to this testimony, she was attracted to Isaac and was willing to
go to him. (*Life-study of Genesis,* pp. 805-806)

Today's Reading

Because of the Spirit's testimony, we have all been attracted
to Christ. Every saved one who loves and seeks the Lord has
been attracted in this way....We enjoy coming to the church
meetings and telling the Lord Jesus how much we love Him. Oh,
we love Him, we seek Him, and we praise Him!

The Spirit also convinces the bride (Gen. 24:54-58). After the servant, typifying the Spirit, brought Rebekah the riches, she was convinced and was willing to marry Isaac. Although her relatives wanted her to linger, Rebekah, upon hearing the servant's testimony of Isaac, said, "I will go" (v. 58). She was willing to go to Isaac in the land of Canaan. Likewise, we are willing to go to Christ. Although we have never seen Him, we have been attracted by Him and we love Him (1 Pet. 1:8). Although Rebekah had never met Isaac, she loved him. When she heard about him, she simply loved him and wanted to go to a land far off to be with him.

Eventually, the servant brought Rebekah to Isaac (Gen. 24:51, 61-67). Although it was a long journey, he brought her through and presented her to Isaac as his bride. The Holy Spirit has convinced us, and now He is bringing us to Christ. Although it is a long journey, eventually He will bring us through and present us to Christ as His lovely bride.

Isaac received Rebekah in the evening (vv. 63-64). This implies that the marriage of Christ will be in the evening of the age. At the close of this age, Christ will come to meet His bride.

Isaac brought Rebekah into his mother Sarah's tent and loved her (v. 67). As we have seen, Sarah typifies grace. Hence, this means that Christ will meet us in grace as well as in love.

This chapter ends with the words, "Isaac was comforted after his mother's death." If I had been the writer, I would have said that Rebekah was comforted after her long journey. But the Bible does not say this. Do not consider your comfort, your satisfaction; rather, consider Christ's comfort, Christ's satisfaction. If Christ has no comfort and satisfaction, we cannot have any comfort and satisfaction either. Our satisfaction depends on His. Our comfort is His comfort, and His satisfaction is ours. Christ is now waiting for His comfort. When will He have it? On the day of His marriage. That day will come. (*Life-study of Genesis,* pp. 806-807, 811)

Further Reading: Life-study of Genesis, msg. 61; *The Spirit with Our Spirit,* ch. 12

Enlightenment and inspiration: _____

_____
_____
_____

Hymns, #170

1   Lord, Thou art the lovely Bridegroom,
        God appointed, dear to us;
    Thy dear self is so attractive,
        To our heart so beauteous!

2   Dear Beloved, we admire Thee,
        Who can tell Thy preciousness;
    All Thy love we deeply treasure
        And Thine untold loveliness.

3   Thou art fairer than the fairest,
        Thou art sweeter than the sweet;
    Thou art meek and Thou art gracious,
        None can e'er with Thee compete.

4   Full of myrrh are all Thy garments,
        And Thy lips are filled with grace;
    In the savor of Thy suffering,
        We in love Thyself embrace.

5   It is with the oil of gladness
        Thy God hath anointed Thee;
    From the palaces of ivory
        Praise shall ever rise to Thee.

6   God hath blessed Thee, Lord, forever,
        Thou hast won the victory;
    Now we see Thee throned in glory
        With Thy pow'r and majesty.

7   Thou art the desire of nations,
        All Thy worth they'll ever prove;
    Thou, the chiefest of ten thousand,
        Ever worthy of our love.

Composition for prophecy with main point and sub-points: _____

_____

_____

_____

_____

_____

_____

_____

_____

_____

_____

_____

_____

_____

_____

_____

_____

_____

_____

_____

_____

_____

_____

_____

_____

_____

_____

_____

_____

_____

_____

_____

_____

_____

Reading Schedule for the Recovery Version of the Old Testament with Footnotes

Wk.	Lord's Day	Monday	Tuesday	Wednesday	Thursday	Friday	Saturday
1	Gen. 1:1-5 ☐	1:6-23 ☐	1:24-31 ☐	2:1-9 ☐	2:10-25 ☐	3:1-13 ☐	3:14-24 ☐
2	4:1-26 ☐	5:1-32 ☐	6:1-22 ☐	7:1—8:3 ☐	8:4-22 ☐	9:1-29 ☐	10:1-32 ☐
3	11:1-32 ☐	12:1-20 ☐	13:1-18 ☐	14:1-24 ☐	15:1-21 ☐	16:1-16 ☐	17:1-27 ☐
4	18:1-33 ☐	19:1-38 ☐	20:1-18 ☐	21:1-34 ☐	22:1-24 ☐	23:1—24:27 ☐	24:28-67 ☐
5	25:1-34 ☐	26:1-35 ☐	27:1-46 ☐	28:1-22 ☐	29:1-35 ☐	30:1-43 ☐	31:1-55 ☐
6	32:1-32 ☐	33:1—34:31 ☐	35:1-29 ☐	36:1-43 ☐	37:1-36 ☐	38:1—39:23 ☐	40:1—41:13 ☐
7	41:14-57 ☐	42:1-38 ☐	43:1-34 ☐	44:1-34 ☐	45:1-28 ☐	46:1-34 ☐	47:1-31 ☐
8	48:1-22 ☐	49:1-15 ☐	49:16-33 ☐	50:1-26 ☐	Exo. 1:1-22 ☐	2:1-25 ☐	3:1-22 ☐
9	4:1-31 ☐	5:1-23 ☐	6:1-30 ☐	7:1-25 ☐	8:1-32 ☐	9:1-35 ☐	10:1-29 ☐
10	11:1-10 ☐	12:1-14 ☐	12:15-36 ☐	12:37-51 ☐	13:1-22 ☐	14:1-31 ☐	15:1-27 ☐
11	16:1-36 ☐	17:1-16 ☐	18:1-27 ☐	19:1-25 ☐	20:1-26 ☐	21:1-36 ☐	22:1-31 ☐
12	23:1-33 ☐	24:1-18 ☐	25:1-22 ☐	25:23-40 ☐	26:1-14 ☐	26:15-37 ☐	27:1-21 ☐
13	28:1-21 ☐	28:22-43 ☐	29:1-21 ☐	29:22-46 ☐	30:1-10 ☐	30:11-38 ☐	31:1-17 ☐
14	31:18—32:35 ☐	33:1-23 ☐	34:1-35 ☐	35:1-35 ☐	36:1-38 ☐	37:1-29 ☐	38:1-31 ☐
15	39:1-43 ☐	40:1-38 ☐	Lev. 1:1-17 ☐	2:1-16 ☐	3:1-17 ☐	4:1-35 ☐	5:1-19 ☐
16	6:1-30 ☐	7:1-38 ☐	8:1-36 ☐	9:1-24 ☐	10:1-20 ☐	11:1-47 ☐	12:1-8 ☐
17	13:1-28 ☐	13:29-59 ☐	14:1-18 ☐	14:19-32 ☐	14:33-57 ☐	15:1-33 ☐	16:1-17 ☐
18	16:18-34 ☐	17:1-16 ☐	18:1-30 ☐	19:1-37 ☐	20:1-27 ☐	21:1-24 ☐	22:1-33 ☐
19	23:1-22 ☐	23:23-44 ☐	24:1-23 ☐	25:1-23 ☐	25:24-55 ☐	26:1-24 ☐	26:25-46 ☐
20	27:1-34 ☐	Num. 1:1-54 ☐	2:1-34 ☐	3:1-51 ☐	4:1-49 ☐	5:1-31 ☐	6:1-27 ☐
21	7:1-41 ☐	7:42-88 ☐	7:89—8:26 ☐	9:1-23 ☐	10:1-36 ☐	11:1-35 ☐	12:1—13:33 ☐
22	14:1-45 ☐	15:1-41 ☐	16:1-50 ☐	17:1—18:7 ☐	18:8-32 ☐	19:1-22 ☐	20:1-29 ☐
23	21:1-35 ☐	22:1-41 ☐	23:1-30 ☐	24:1-25 ☐	25:1-18 ☐	26:1-65 ☐	27:1-23 ☐
24	28:1-31 ☐	29:1-40 ☐	30:1—31:24 ☐	31:25-54 ☐	32:1-42 ☐	33:1-56 ☐	34:1-29 ☐
25	35:1-34 ☐	36:1-13 ☐	Deut. 1:1-46 ☐	2:1-37 ☐	3:1-29 ☐	4:1-49 ☐	5:1-33 ☐
26	6:1—7:26 ☐	8:1-20 ☐	9:1-29 ☐	10:1-22 ☐	11:1-32 ☐	12:1-32 ☐	13:1—14:21 ☐

Reading Schedule for the Recovery Version of the Old Testament with Footnotes

Wk.	Lord's Day	Monday	Tuesday	Wednesday	Thursday	Friday	Saturday
27	14:22—15:23 ☐	16:1-22 ☐	17:1—18:8 ☐	18:9—19:21 ☐	20:1—21:17 ☐	21:18—22:30 ☐	23:1-25 ☐
28	24:1-22 ☐	25:1-19 ☐	26:1-19 ☐	27:1-26 ☐	28:1-68 ☐	29:1-29 ☐	30:1—31:29 ☐
29	31:30—32:52 ☐	33:1-29 ☐	34:1-12 ☐	Josh. 1:1-18 ☐	2:1-24 ☐	3:1-17 ☐	4:1-24 ☐
30	5:1-15 ☐	6:1-27 ☐	7:1-26 ☐	8:1-35 ☐	9:1-27 ☐	10:1-43 ☐	11:1—12:24 ☐
31	13:1-33 ☐	14:1—15:63 ☐	16:1—18:28 ☐	19:1-51 ☐	20:1—21:45 ☐	22:1-34 ☐	23:1—24:33 ☐
32	Judg. 1:1-36 ☐	2:1-23 ☐	3:1-31 ☐	4:1-24 ☐	5:1-31 ☐	6:1-40 ☐	7:1-25 ☐
33	8:1-35 ☐	9:1-57 ☐	10:1—11:40 ☐	12:1—13:25 ☐	14:1—15:20 ☐	16:1-31 ☐	17:1—18:31 ☐
34	19:1-30 ☐	20:1-48 ☐	21:1-25 ☐	Ruth 1:1-22 ☐	2:1-23 ☐	3:1-18 ☐	4:1-22 ☐
35	1 Sam. 1:1-28 ☐	2:1-36 ☐	3:1—4:22 ☐	5:1—6:21 ☐	7:1—8:22 ☐	9:1-27 ☐	10:1—11:15 ☐
36	12:1—13:23 ☐	14:1-52 ☐	15:1-35 ☐	16:1-23 ☐	17:1-58 ☐	18:1-30 ☐	19:1-24 ☐
37	20:1-42 ☐	21:1—22:23 ☐	23:1—24:22 ☐	25:1-44 ☐	26:1-25 ☐	27:1—28:25 ☐	29:1—30:31 ☐
38	31:1-13 ☐	2 Sam. 1:1-27 ☐	2:1-32 ☐	3:1-39 ☐	4:1—5:25 ☐	6:1-23 ☐	7:1-29 ☐
39	8:1—9:13 ☐	10:1—11:27 ☐	12:1-31 ☐	13:1-39 ☐	14:1-33 ☐	15:1—16:23 ☐	17:1—18:33 ☐
40	19:1-43 ☐	20:1—21:22 ☐	22:1-51 ☐	23:1-39 ☐	24:1-25 ☐	1 Kings 1:1-19 ☐	1:20-53 ☐
41	2:1-46 ☐	3:1-28 ☐	4:1-34 ☐	5:1—6:38 ☐	7:1-22 ☐	7:23-51 ☐	8:1-36 ☐
42	8:37-66 ☐	9:1-28 ☐	10:1-29 ☐	11:1-43 ☐	12:1-33 ☐	13:1-34 ☐	14:1-31 ☐
43	15:1-34 ☐	16:1—17:24 ☐	18:1-46 ☐	19:1-21 ☐	20:1-43 ☐	21:1—22:53 ☐	2 Kings 1:1-18 ☐
44	2:1—3:27 ☐	4:1-44 ☐	5:1—6:33 ☐	7:1-20 ☐	8:1-29 ☐	9:1-37 ☐	10:1-36 ☐
45	11:1—12:21 ☐	13:1—14:29 ☐	15:1-38 ☐	16:1-20 ☐	17:1-41 ☐	18:1-37 ☐	19:1-37 ☐
46	20:1—21:26 ☐	22:1-20 ☐	23:1-37 ☐	24:1—25:30 ☐	1 Chron. 1:1-54 ☐	2:1—3:24 ☐	4:1—5:26 ☐
47	6:1-81 ☐	7:1-40 ☐	8:1-40 ☐	9:1-44 ☐	10:1—11:47 ☐	12:1-40 ☐	13:1—14:17 ☐
48	15:1—16:43 ☐	17:1-27 ☐	18:1—19:19 ☐	20:1—21:30 ☐	22:1—23:32 ☐	24:1—25:31 ☐	26:1-32 ☐
49	27:1-34 ☐	28:1—29:30 ☐	2 Chron. 1:1-17 ☐	2:1—3:17 ☐	4:1—5:14 ☐	6:1-42 ☐	7:1—8:18 ☐
50	9:1—10:19 ☐	11:1—12:16 ☐	13:1—15:19 ☐	16:1—17:19 ☐	18:1—19:11 ☐	20:1-37 ☐	21:1—22:12 ☐
51	23:1—24:27 ☐	25:1—26:23 ☐	27:1—28:27 ☐	29:1-36 ☐	30:1—31:21 ☐	32:1-33 ☐	33:1—34:33 ☐
52	35:1—36:23 ☐	Ezra 1:1-11 ☐	2:1-70 ☐	3:1—4:24 ☐	5:1—6:22 ☐	7:1-28 ☐	8:1-36 ☐

Reading Schedule for the Recovery Version of the Old Testament with Footnotes

Wk.	Lord's Day	Monday	Tuesday	Wednesday	Thursday	Friday	Saturday
53	9:1—10:44 ☐	Neh. 1:1-11 ☐	2:1—3:32 ☐	4:1—5:19 ☐	6:1-19 ☐	7:1-73 ☐	8:1-18 ☐
54	9:1-20 ☐	9:21-38 ☐	10:1—11:36 ☐	12:1-47 ☐	13:1-31 ☐	Esth. 1:1-22 ☐	2:1—3:15 ☐
55	4:1—5:14 ☐	6:1—7:10 ☐	8:1-17 ☐	9:1—10:3 ☐	Job 1:1-22 ☐	2:1—3:26 ☐	4:1—5:27 ☐
56	6:1—7:21 ☐	8:1—9:35 ☐	10:1—11:20 ☐	12:1—13:28 ☐	14:1—15:35 ☐	16:1—17:16 ☐	18:1—19:29 ☐
57	20:1—21:34 ☐	22:1—23:17 ☐	24:1—25:6 ☐	26:1—27:23 ☐	28:1—29:25 ☐	30:1—31:40 ☐	32:1—33:33 ☐
58	34:1—35:16 ☐	36:1-33 ☐	37:1-24 ☐	38:1-41 ☐	39:1-30 ☐	40:1-24 ☐	41:1-34 ☐
59	42:1-17 ☐	Psa. 1:1-6 ☐	2:1—3:8 ☐	4:1—6:10 ☐	7:1—8:9 ☐	9:1—10:18 ☐	11:1—15:5 ☐
60	16:1—17:15 ☐	18:1-50 ☐	19:1—21:13 ☐	22:1-31 ☐	23:1—24:10 ☐	25:1—27:14 ☐	28:1—30:12 ☐
61	31:1—32:11 ☐	33:1—34:22 ☐	35:1—36:12 ☐	37:1-40 ☐	38:1—39:13 ☐	40:1—41:13 ☐	42:1—43:5 ☐
62	44:1-26 ☐	45:1-17 ☐	46:1—48:14 ☐	49:1—50:23 ☐	51:1—52:9 ☐	53:1—55:23 ☐	56:1—58:11 ☐
63	59:1—61:8 ☐	62:1—64:10 ☐	65:1—67:7 ☐	68:1-35 ☐	69:1—70:5 ☐	71:1—72:20 ☐	73:1—74:23 ☐
64	75:1—77:20 ☐	78:1-72 ☐	79:1—81:16 ☐	82:1—84:12 ☐	85:1—87:7 ☐	88:1—89:52 ☐	90:1—91:16 ☐
65	92:1—94:23 ☐	95:1—97:12 ☐	98:1—101:8 ☐	102:1—103:22 ☐	104:1—105:45 ☐	106:1-48 ☐	107:1-43 ☐
66	108:1—109:31 ☐	110:1—112:10 ☐	113:1—115:18 ☐	116:1—118:29 ☐	119:1-32 ☐	119:33-72 ☐	119:73-120 ☐
67	119:121-176 ☐	120:1—124:8 ☐	125:1—128:6 ☐	129:1—132:18 ☐	133:1—135:21 ☐	136:1—138:8 ☐	139:1—140:13 ☐
68	141:1—144:15 ☐	145:1—147:20 ☐	148:1—150:6 ☐	Prov. 1:1-33 ☐	2:1—3:35 ☐	4:1—5:23 ☐	6:1-35 ☐
69	7:1—8:36 ☐	9:1—10:32 ☐	11:1—12:28 ☐	13:1—14:35 ☐	15:1-33 ☐	16:1-33 ☐	17:1-28 ☐
70	18:1-24 ☐	19:1—20:30 ☐	21:1—22:29 ☐	23:1-35 ☐	24:1—25:28 ☐	26:1—27:27 ☐	28:1—29:27 ☐
71	30:1-33 ☐	31:1-31 ☐	Eccl. 1:1-18 ☐	2:1—3:22 ☐	4:1—5:20 ☐	6:1—7:29 ☐	8:1—9:18 ☐
72	10:1—11:10 ☐	12:1-14 ☐	S.S. 1:1-8 ☐	1:9-17 ☐	2:1-17 ☐	3:1-11 ☐	4:1-8 ☐
73	4:9-16 ☐	5:1-16 ☐	6:1-13 ☐	7:1-13 ☐	8:1-14 ☐	Isa. 1:1-11 ☐	1:12-31 ☐
74	2:1-22 ☐	3:1-26 ☐	4:1-6 ☐	5:1-30 ☐	6:1-13 ☐	7:1-25 ☐	8:1-22 ☐
75	9:1-21 ☐	10:1-34 ☐	11:1—12:6 ☐	13:1-22 ☐	14:1-14 ☐	14:15-32 ☐	15:1—16:14 ☐
76	17:1—18:7 ☐	19:1-25 ☐	20:1—21:17 ☐	22:1-25 ☐	23:1-18 ☐	24:1-23 ☐	25:1-12 ☐
77	26:1-21 ☐	27:1-13 ☐	28:1-29 ☐	29:1-24 ☐	30:1-33 ☐	31:1—32:20 ☐	33:1-24 ☐
78	34:1-17 ☐	35:1-10 ☐	36:1-22 ☐	37:1-38 ☐	38:1—39:8 ☐	40:1-31 ☐	41:1-29 ☐

Reading Schedule for the Recovery Version of the Old Testament with Footnotes

Wk.	Lord's Day	Monday	Tuesday	Wednesday	Thursday	Friday	Saturday
79	42:1-25	43:1-28	44:1-28	45:1-25	46:1-13	47:1-15	48:1-22
80	49:1-13	49:14-26	50:1—51:23	52:1-15	53:1-12	54:1-17	55:1-13
81	56:1-12	57:1-21	58:1-14	59:1-21	60:1-22	61:1-11	62:1-12
82	63:1-19	64:1-12	65:1-25	66:1-24	Jer. 1:1-19	2:1-19	2:20-37
83	3:1-25	4:1-31	5:1-31	6:1-30	7:1-34	8:1-22	9:1-26
84	10:1-25	11:1—12:17	13:1-27	14:1-22	15:1-21	16:1—17:27	18:1-23
85	19:1—20:18	21:1—22:30	23:1-40	24:1—25:38	26:1—27:22	28:1—29:32	30:1-24
86	31:1-23	31:24-40	32:1-44	33:1-26	34:1-22	35:1-19	36:1-32
87	37:1-21	38:1-28	39:1—40:16	41:1—42:22	43:1—44:30	45:1—46:28	47:1—48:16
88	48:17-47	49:1-22	49:23-39	50:1-27	50:28-46	51:1-27	51:28-64
89	52:1-34	Lam. 1:1-22	2:1-22	3:1-39	3:40-66	4:1-22	5:1-22
90	Ezek. 1:1-14	1:15-28	2:1—3:27	4:1—5:17	6:1—7:27	8:1—9:11	10:1—11:25
91	12:1—13:23	14:1—15:8	16:1-63	17:1—18:32	19:1-14	20:1-49	21:1-32
92	22:1-31	23:1-49	24:1-27	25:1—26:21	27:1-36	28:1-26	29:1—30:26
93	31:1—32:32	33:1-33	34:1-31	35:1—36:21	36:22-38	37:1-28	38:1—39:29
94	40:1-27	40:28-49	41:1-26	42:1—43:27	44:1-31	45:1-25	46:1-24
95	47:1-23	48:1-35	Dan. 1:1-21	2:1-30	2:31-49	3:1-30	4:1-37
96	5:1-31	6:1-28	7:1-12	7:13-28	8:1-27	9:1-27	10:1-21
97	11:1-22	11:23-45	12:1-13	Hosea 1:1-11	2:1-23	3:1—4:19	5:1-15
98	6:1-11	7:1-16	8:1-14	9:1-17	10:1-15	11:1-12	12:1-14
99	13:1—14:9	Joel 1:1-20	2:1-16	2:17-32	3:1-21	Amos 1:1-15	2:1-16
100	3:1-15	4:1—5:27	6:1—7:17	8:1—9:15	Obad. 1-21	Jonah 1:1-17	2:1—4:11
101	Micah 1:1-16	2:1—3:12	4:1—5:15	6:1—7:20	Nahum 1:1-15	2:1—3:19	Hab. 1:1-17
102	2:1-20	3:1-19	Zeph. 1:1-18	2:1-15	3:1-20	Hag. 1:1-15	2:1-23
103	Zech. 1:1-21	2:1-13	3:1-10	4:1-14	5:1—6:15	7:1—8:23	9:1-17
104	10:1—11:17	12:1—13:9	14:1-21	Mal. 1:1-14	2:1-17	3:1-18	4:1-6

Reading Schedule for the Recovery Version of the New Testament with Footnotes

Wk.	Lord's Day	Monday	Tuesday	Wednesday	Thursday	Friday	Saturday
1	Matt. 1:1-2 ☐	1:3-7 ☐	1:8-17 ☐	1:18-25 ☐	2:1-23 ☐	3:1-6 ☐	3:7-17 ☐
2	4:1-11 ☐	4:12-25 ☐	5:1-4 ☐	5:5-12 ☐	5:13-20 ☐	5:21-26 ☐	5:27-48 ☐
3	6:1-8 ☐	6:9-18 ☐	6:19-34 ☐	7:1-12 ☐	7:13-29 ☐	8:1-13 ☐	8:14-22 ☐
4	8:23-34 ☐	9:1-13 ☐	9:14-17 ☐	9:18-34 ☐	9:35—10:5 ☐	10:6-25 ☐	10:26-42 ☐
5	11:1-15 ☐	11:16-30 ☐	12:1-14 ☐	12:15-32 ☐	12:33-42 ☐	12:43—13:2 ☐	13:3-12 ☐
6	13:13-30 ☐	13:31-43 ☐	13:44-58 ☐	14:1-13 ☐	14:14-21 ☐	14:22-36 ☐	15:1-20 ☐
7	15:21-31 ☐	15:32-39 ☐	16:1-12 ☐	16:13-20 ☐	16:21-28 ☐	17:1-13 ☐	17:14-27 ☐
8	18:1-14 ☐	18:15-22 ☐	18:23-35 ☐	19:1-15 ☐	19:16-30 ☐	20:1-16 ☐	20:17-34 ☐
9	21:1-11 ☐	21:12-22 ☐	21:23-32 ☐	21:33-46 ☐	22:1-22 ☐	22:23-33 ☐	22:34-46 ☐
10	23:1-12 ☐	23:13-39 ☐	24:1-14 ☐	24:15-31 ☐	24:32-51 ☐	25:1-13 ☐	25:14-30 ☐
11	25:31-46 ☐	26:1-16 ☐	26:17-35 ☐	26:36-46 ☐	26:47-64 ☐	26:65-75 ☐	27:1-26 ☐
12	27:27-44 ☐	27:45-56 ☐	27:57—28:15 ☐	28:16-20 ☐	Mark 1:1 ☐	1:2-6 ☐	1:7-13 ☐
13	1:14-28 ☐	1:29-45 ☐	2:1-12 ☐	2:13-28 ☐	3:1-19 ☐	3:20-35 ☐	4:1-25 ☐
14	4:26-41 ☐	5:1-20 ☐	5:21-43 ☐	6:1-29 ☐	6:30-56 ☐	7:1-23 ☐	7:24-37 ☐
15	8:1-26 ☐	8:27—9:1 ☐	9:2-29 ☐	9:30-50 ☐	10:1-16 ☐	10:17-34 ☐	10:35-52 ☐
16	11:1-16 ☐	11:17-33 ☐	12:1-27 ☐	12:28-44 ☐	13:1-13 ☐	13:14-37 ☐	14:1-26 ☐
17	14:27-52 ☐	14:53-72 ☐	15:1-15 ☐	15:16-47 ☐	16:1-8 ☐	16:9-20 ☐	Luke 1:1-4 ☐
18	1:5-25 ☐	1:26-46 ☐	1:47-56 ☐	1:57-80 ☐	2:1-8 ☐	2:9-20 ☐	2:21-39 ☐
19	2:40-52 ☐	3:1-20 ☐	3:21-38 ☐	4:1-13 ☐	4:14-30 ☐	4:31-44 ☐	5:1-26 ☐
20	5:27—6:16 ☐	6:17-38 ☐	6:39-49 ☐	7:1-17 ☐	7:18-23 ☐	7:24-35 ☐	7:36-50 ☐
21	8:1-15 ☐	8:16-25 ☐	8:26-39 ☐	8:40-56 ☐	9:1-17 ☐	9:18-26 ☐	9:27-36 ☐
22	9:37-50 ☐	9:51-62 ☐	10:1-11 ☐	10:12-24 ☐	10:25-37 ☐	10:38-42 ☐	11:1-13 ☐
23	11:14-26 ☐	11:27-36 ☐	11:37-54 ☐	12:1-12 ☐	12:13-21 ☐	12:22-34 ☐	12:35-48 ☐
24	12:49-59 ☐	13:1-9 ☐	13:10-17 ☐	13:18-30 ☐	13:31—14:6 ☐	14:7-14 ☐	14:15-24 ☐
25	14:25-35 ☐	15:1-10 ☐	15:11-21 ☐	15:22-32 ☐	16:1-13 ☐	16:14-22 ☐	16:23-31 ☐
26	17:1-19 ☐	17:20-37 ☐	18:1-14 ☐	18:15-30 ☐	18:31-43 ☐	19:1-10 ☐	19:11-27 ☐

Reading Schedule for the Recovery Version of the New Testament with Footnotes

Wk.	Lord's Day	Monday	Tuesday	Wednesday	Thursday	Friday	Saturday
27	Luke 19:28-48 ☐	20:1-19 ☐	20:20-38 ☐	20:39—21:4 ☐	21:5-27 ☐	21:28-38 ☐	22:1-20 ☐
28	22:21-38 ☐	22:39-54 ☐	22:55-71 ☐	23:1-43 ☐	23:44-56 ☐	24:1-12 ☐	24:13-35 ☐
29	24:36-53 ☐	John 1:1-13 ☐	1:14-18 ☐	1:19-34 ☐	1:35-51 ☐	2:1-11 ☐	2:12-22 ☐
30	2:23—3:13 ☐	3:14-21 ☐	3:22-36 ☐	4:1-14 ☐	4:15-26 ☐	4:27-42 ☐	4:43-54 ☐
31	5:1-16 ☐	5:17-30 ☐	5:31-47 ☐	6:1-15 ☐	6:16-31 ☐	6:32-51 ☐	6:52-71 ☐
32	7:1-9 ☐	7:10-24 ☐	7:25-36 ☐	7:37-52 ☐	7:53—8:11 ☐	8:12-27 ☐	8:28-44 ☐
33	8:45-59 ☐	9:1-13 ☐	9:14-34 ☐	9:35—10:9 ☐	10:10-30 ☐	10:31—11:4 ☐	11:5-22 ☐
34	11:23-40 ☐	11:41-57 ☐	12:1-11 ☐	12:12-24 ☐	12:25-36 ☐	12:37-50 ☐	13:1-11 ☐
35	13:12-30 ☐	13:31-38 ☐	14:1-6 ☐	14:7-20 ☐	14:21-31 ☐	15:1-11 ☐	15:12-27 ☐
36	16:1-15 ☐	16:16-33 ☐	17:1-5 ☐	17:6-13 ☐	17:14-24 ☐	17:25—18:11 ☐	18:12-27 ☐
37	18:28-40 ☐	19:1-16 ☐	19:17-30 ☐	19:31-42 ☐	20:1-13 ☐	20:14-18 ☐	20:19-22 ☐
38	20:23-31 ☐	21:1-14 ☐	21:15-22 ☐	21:23-25 ☐	Acts 1:1-8 ☐	1:9-14 ☐	1:15-26 ☐
39	2:1-13 ☐	2:14-21 ☐	2:22-36 ☐	2:37-41 ☐	2:42-47 ☐	3:1-18 ☐	3:19—4:22 ☐
40	4:23-37 ☐	5:1-16 ☐	5:17-32 ☐	5:33-42 ☐	6:1—7:1 ☐	7:2-29 ☐	7:30-60 ☐
41	8:1-13 ☐	8:14-25 ☐	8:26-40 ☐	9:1-19 ☐	9:20-43 ☐	10:1-16 ☐	10:17-33 ☐
42	10:34-48 ☐	11:1-18 ☐	11:19-30 ☐	12:1-25 ☐	13:1-12 ☐	13:13-43 ☐	13:44—14:5 ☐
43	14:6-28 ☐	15:1-12 ☐	15:13-34 ☐	15:35—16:5 ☐	16:6-18 ☐	16:19-40 ☐	17:1-18 ☐
44	17:19-34 ☐	18:1-17 ☐	18:18-28 ☐	19:1-20 ☐	19:21-41 ☐	20:1-12 ☐	20:13-38 ☐
45	21:1-14 ☐	21:15-26 ☐	21:27-40 ☐	22:1-21 ☐	22:22-29 ☐	22:30—23:11 ☐	23:12-15 ☐
46	23:16-30 ☐	23:31—24:21 ☐	24:22—25:5 ☐	25:6-27 ☐	26:1-13 ☐	26:14-32 ☐	27:1-26 ☐
47	27:27—28:10 ☐	28:11-22 ☐	28:23-31 ☐	Rom. 1:1-2 ☐	1:3-7 ☐	1:8-17 ☐	1:18-25 ☐
48	1:26—2:10 ☐	2:11-29 ☐	3:1-20 ☐	3:21-31 ☐	4:1-12 ☐	4:13-25 ☐	5:1-11 ☐
49	5:12-17 ☐	5:18—6:5 ☐	6:6-11 ☐	6:12-23 ☐	7:1-12 ☐	7:13-25 ☐	8:1-2 ☐
50	8:3-6 ☐	8:7-13 ☐	8:14-25 ☐	8:26-39 ☐	9:1-18 ☐	9:19—10:3 ☐	10:4-15 ☐
51	10:16—11:10 ☐	11:11-22 ☐	11:23-36 ☐	12:1-3 ☐	12:4-21 ☐	13:1-14 ☐	14:1-12 ☐
52	14:13-23 ☐	15:1-13 ☐	15:14-33 ☐	16:1-5 ☐	16:6-24 ☐	16:25-27 ☐	1 Cor. 1:1-4 ☐

Reading Schedule for the Recovery Version of the New Testament with Footnotes

Wk.	Lord's Day	Monday	Tuesday	Wednesday	Thursday	Friday	Saturday
53	1 Cor. 1:5-9 ☐	1:10-17 ☐	1:18-31 ☐	2:1-5 ☐	2:6-10 ☐	2:11-16 ☐	3:1-9 ☐
54	3:10-13 ☐	3:14-23 ☐	4:1-9 ☐	4:10-21 ☐	5:1-13 ☐	6:1-11 ☐	6:12-20 ☐
55	7:1-16 ☐	7:17-24 ☐	7:25-40 ☐	8:1-13 ☐	9:1-15 ☐	9:16-27 ☐	10:1-4 ☐
56	10:5-13 ☐	10:14-33 ☐	11:1-6 ☐	11:7-16 ☐	11:17-26 ☐	11:27-34 ☐	12:1-11 ☐
57	12:12-22 ☐	12:23-31 ☐	13:1-13 ☐	14:1-12 ☐	14:13-25 ☐	14:26-33 ☐	14:34-40 ☐
58	15:1-19 ☐	15:20-28 ☐	15:29-34 ☐	15:35-49 ☐	15:50-58 ☐	16:1-9 ☐	16:10-24 ☐
59	2 Cor. 1:1-4 ☐	1:5-14 ☐	1:15-22 ☐	1:23—2:11 ☐	2:12-17 ☐	3:1-6 ☐	3:7-11 ☐
60	3:12-18 ☐	4:1-6 ☐	4:7-12 ☐	4:13-18 ☐	5:1-8 ☐	5:9-15 ☐	5:16-21 ☐
61	6:1-13 ☐	6:14—7:4 ☐	7:5-16 ☐	8:1-15 ☐	8:16-24 ☐	9:1-15 ☐	10:1-6 ☐
62	10:7-18 ☐	11:1-15 ☐	11:16-33 ☐	12:1-10 ☐	12:11-21 ☐	13:1-10 ☐	13:11-14 ☐
63	Gal. 1:1-5 ☐	1:6-14 ☐	1:15-24 ☐	2:1-13 ☐	2:14-21 ☐	3:1-4 ☐	3:5-14 ☐
64	3:15-22 ☐	3:23-29 ☐	4:1-7 ☐	4:8-20 ☐	4:21-31 ☐	5:1-12 ☐	5:13-21 ☐
65	5:22-26 ☐	6:1-10 ☐	6:11-15 ☐	6:16-18 ☐	Eph. 1:1-3 ☐	1:4-6 ☐	1:7-10 ☐
66	1:11-14 ☐	1:15-18 ☐	1:19-23 ☐	2:1-5 ☐	2:6-10 ☐	2:11-14 ☐	2:15-18 ☐
67	2:19-22 ☐	3:1-7 ☐	3:8-13 ☐	3:14-18 ☐	3:19-21 ☐	4:1-4 ☐	4:5-10 ☐
68	4:11-16 ☐	4:17-24 ☐	4:25-32 ☐	5:1-10 ☐	5:11-21 ☐	5:22-26 ☐	5:27-33 ☐
69	6:1-9 ☐	6:10-14 ☐	6:15-18 ☐	6:19-24 ☐	Phil. 1:1-7 ☐	1:8-18 ☐	1:19-26 ☐
70	1:27—2:4 ☐	2:5-11 ☐	2:12-16 ☐	2:17-30 ☐	3:1-6 ☐	3:7-11 ☐	3:12-16 ☐
71	3:17-21 ☐	4:1-9 ☐	4:10-23 ☐	Col. 1:1-8 ☐	1:9-13 ☐	1:14-23 ☐	1:24-29 ☐
72	2:1-7 ☐	2:8-15 ☐	2:16-23 ☐	3:1-4 ☐	3:5-15 ☐	3:16-25 ☐	4:1-18 ☐
73	1 Thes. 1:1-3 ☐	1:4-10 ☐	2:1-12 ☐	2:13—3:5 ☐	3:6-13 ☐	4:1-10 ☐	4:11—5:11 ☐
74	5:12-28 ☐	2 Thes. 1:1-12 ☐	2:1-17 ☐	3:1-18 ☐	1 Tim. 1:1-2 ☐	1:3-4 ☐	1:5-14 ☐
75	1:15-20 ☐	2:1-7 ☐	2:8-15 ☐	3:1-13 ☐	3:14—4:5 ☐	4:6-16 ☐	5:1-25 ☐
76	6:1-10 ☐	6:11-21 ☐	2 Tim. 1:1-10 ☐	1:11-18 ☐	2:1-15 ☐	2:16-26 ☐	3:1-13 ☐
77	3:14—4:8 ☐	4:9-22 ☐	Titus 1:1-4 ☐	1:5-16 ☐	2:1-15 ☐	3:1-8 ☐	3:9-15 ☐
78	Philem. 1:1-11 ☐	1:12-25 ☐	Heb. 1:1-2 ☐	1:3-5 ☐	1:6-14 ☐	2:1-9 ☐	2:10-18 ☐

Reading Schedule for the Recovery Version of the New Testament with Footnotes

Wk.	Lord's Day	Monday	Tuesday	Wednesday	Thursday	Friday	Saturday
79	Heb. 3:1-6 ☐	3:7-19 ☐	4:1-9 ☐	4:10-13 ☐	4:14-16 ☐	5:1-10 ☐	5:11—6:3 ☐
80	6:4-8 ☐	6:9-20 ☐	7:1-10 ☐	7:11-28 ☐	8:1-6 ☐	8:7-13 ☐	9:1-4 ☐
81	9:5-14 ☐	9:15-28 ☐	10:1-18 ☐	10:19-28 ☐	10:29-39 ☐	11:1-6 ☐	11:7-19 ☐
82	11:20-31 ☐	11:32-40 ☐	12:1-2 ☐	12:3-13 ☐	12:14-17 ☐	12:18-26 ☐	12:27-29 ☐
83	13:1-7 ☐	13:8-12 ☐	13:13-15 ☐	13:16-25 ☐	James 1:1-8 ☐	1:9-18 ☐	1:19-27 ☐
84	2:1-13 ☐	2:14-26 ☐	3:1-18 ☐	4:1-10 ☐	4:11-17 ☐	5:1-12 ☐	5:13-20 ☐
85	1 Pet. 1:1-2 ☐	1:3-4 ☐	1:5 ☐	1:6-9 ☐	1:10-12 ☐	1:13-17 ☐	1:18-25 ☐
86	2:1-3 ☐	2:4-8 ☐	2:9-17 ☐	2:18-25 ☐	3:1-13 ☐	3:14-22 ☐	4:1-6 ☐
87	4:7-16 ☐	4:17-19 ☐	5:1-4 ☐	5:5-9 ☐	5:10-14 ☐	2 Pet. 1:1-2 ☐	1:3-4 ☐
88	1:5-8 ☐	1:9-11 ☐	1:12-18 ☐	1:19-21 ☐	2:1-3 ☐	2:4-11 ☐	2:12-22 ☐
89	3:1-6 ☐	3:7-9 ☐	3:10-12 ☐	3:13-15 ☐	3:16 ☐	3:17-18 ☐	1 John 1:1-2 ☐
90	1:3-4 ☐	1:5 ☐	1:6 ☐	1:7 ☐	1:8-10 ☐	2:1-2 ☐	2:3-11 ☐
91	2:12-14 ☐	2:15-19 ☐	2:20-23 ☐	2:24-27 ☐	2:28-29 ☐	3:1-5 ☐	3:6-10 ☐
92	3:11-18 ☐	3:19-24 ☐	4:1-6 ☐	4:7-11 ☐	4:12-15 ☐	4:16—5:3 ☐	5:4-13 ☐
93	5:14-17 ☐	5:18-21 ☐	2 John 1:1-3 ☐	1:4-9 ☐	1:10-13 ☐	3 John 1:1-6 ☐	1:7-14 ☐
94	Jude 1:1-4 ☐	1:5-10 ☐	1:11-19 ☐	1:20-25 ☐	Rev. 1:1-3 ☐	1:4-6 ☐	1:7-11 ☐
95	1:12-13 ☐	1:14-16 ☐	1:17-20 ☐	2:1-6 ☐	2:7 ☐	2:8-9 ☐	2:10-11 ☐
96	2:12-14 ☐	2:15-17 ☐	2:18-23 ☐	2:24-29 ☐	3:1-3 ☐	3:4-6 ☐	3:7-9 ☐
97	3:10-13 ☐	3:14-18 ☐	3:19-22 ☐	4:1-5 ☐	4:6-7 ☐	4:8-11 ☐	5:1-6 ☐
98	5:7-14 ☐	6:1-8 ☐	6:9-17 ☐	7:1-8 ☐	7:9-17 ☐	8:1-6 ☐	8:7-12 ☐
99	8:13—9:11 ☐	9:12-21 ☐	10:1-4 ☐	10:5-11 ☐	11:1-4 ☐	11:5-14 ☐	11:15-19 ☐
100	12:1-4 ☐	12:5-9 ☐	12:10-18 ☐	13:1-10 ☐	13:11-18 ☐	14:1-5 ☐	14:6-12 ☐
101	14:13-20 ☐	15:1-8 ☐	16:1-12 ☐	16:13-21 ☐	17:1-6 ☐	17:7-18 ☐	18:1-8 ☐
102	18:9—19:4 ☐	19:5-10 ☐	19:11-16 ☐	19:17-21 ☐	20:1-6 ☐	20:7-10 ☐	20:11-15 ☐
103	21:1 ☐	21:2 ☐	21:3-8 ☐	21:9-13 ☐	21:14-18 ☐	21:19-21 ☐	21:22-27 ☐
104	22:1 ☐	22:2 ☐	22:3-11 ☐	22:12-15 ☐	22:16-17 ☐	22:18-21 ☐	

Week 19 — Day 1　　Today's verses

Gen. And Jehovah appeared to him [Abraham]
18:1-2 by the oaks of Mamre as he was sitting at the entrance of *his* tent....And he lifted up his eyes and looked, and there were three men standing opposite him. And when he saw *them*, he ran from the entrance of the tent to meet them. And he bowed down to the earth.

16 ...Abraham walked with them to send them away.

Date

Week 19 — Day 2　　Today's verses

Gen. Is anything too marvelous for Jehovah? At
18:14 the appointed time I will return to you, according to the time of life, and Sarah shall have a son.

20 And Jehovah said, The cry of Sodom and Gomorrah, how great it is; and their sin, how very heavy it is!

Date

Week 19 — Day 3　　Today's verses

Gen. And Jehovah said, Shall I hide from Abra-
18:17 ham what I am about to do?

22 And the men turned from there and went toward Sodom, while Abraham remained standing before Jehovah.

Date

Week 19 — Day 4　　Today's verses

Gen. Far be it from You to do such a thing, to
18:25 put to death the righteous with the wicked, so that the righteous should be as the wicked. Far be it from You! Shall the Judge of all the earth not do justly?

33 And Jehovah went away as soon as He had finished speaking with Abraham, and Abraham returned to his place.

Date

Week 19 — Day 5　　Today's verses

Gen. Abram dwelt in the land of Canaan, and
13:12 Lot dwelt in the cities of the plain and moved his tent as far as Sodom.

19:1 And the two angels came to Sodom in the evening, and Lot was sitting in the gate of Sodom. And when Lot saw *them*, he rose up to meet them and bowed with his face to the ground.

Date

Week 19 — Day 6　　Today's verses

Gen. But he lingered; so the men seized his
19:16-17 hand and the hand of his wife and the hand of his two daughters, Jehovah being merciful to him, and they brought him out and set him outside the city. And when they had brought them outside, He said, Escape for your life. Do not look behind you....Escape to the hills, lest you be destroyed.

Luke Remember Lot's wife.
17:32

Date

Week 20 — Day 6   Today's verses

Gen.
22:1-2   Now after these things God tested Abraham and said to him, Abraham. And he said, Here I am. And He said, Take now your son, your only son, whom you love, Isaac, and go to the land of Moriah, and offer him there as a burnt offering on one of the mountains of which I will tell you.

8   And Abraham said, God Himself will provide the lamb for a burnt offering, my son...

Week 20 — Day 5   Today's verses

Gen.
17:1-2   And when Abram was ninety-nine years old, Jehovah appeared to Abram and said to him, I am the All-sufficient God; walk before Me, and be perfect. And I will make My covenant between Me and you, and I will multiply you exceedingly.

10   This is My covenant, which you shall keep, between Me and you and your seed after you: Every male among you shall be circumcised.

Week 20 — Day 4   Today's verses

Gen.
15:5-6   And He brought him outside and said, Look now toward the heavens, and count the stars, if you are able to count them. And He said to him, So shall your seed be. And he believed Jehovah, and He accounted it to him as righteousness.

Week 20 — Day 3   Today's verses

Gen.
12:7   And Jehovah appeared to Abram and said, To your seed I will give this land...

13:14-15   And Jehovah said to Abram after Lot had separated from him, Now lift up your eyes, and look from the place where you are, northward and southward and eastward and westward; for all the land that you see I will give to you and to your seed forever.

Week 20 — Day 2   Today's verses

Gal.
3:8   And the Scripture, foreseeing that God would justify the Gentiles out of faith, announced the gospel beforehand to Abraham: "In you shall all the nations be blessed."

14   In order that the blessing of Abraham might come to the Gentiles in Christ Jesus, that we might receive the promise of the Spirit through faith.

Week 20 — Day 1   Today's verses

Acts
7:2-4   ...The God of glory appeared to our father Abraham while he was in Mesopotamia, before he dwelt in Haran, and said to him, "Come out from your land and from your relatives, and come into the land which I will show you." Then he came forth from the land of the Chaldeans and dwelt in Haran. And from there, after his father died, He removed him into this land, in which you now dwell.

Week 21 — Day 4   Today's verses

Heb. Let us therefore come forward with bold-
4:16 ness to the throne of grace that we may receive mercy and find grace for timely
help.

Rev. And he showed me a river of water of life,
22:1 bright as crystal, proceeding out of the
throne of God and of the Lamb in the middle of its street.

Date

Week 21 — Day 5   Today's verses

Gen. And Sarah my master's wife bore a son to
24:36 my master after she had become old. And
he has given all that he has to him.

22:9 And they came to the place of which God
had told him. And Abraham built the altar
there and laid the wood in order and
bound Isaac his son and laid him on the
altar on top of the wood.

Date

Week 21 — Day 6   Today's verses

Gen. And Jehovah appeared to him the same
26:24-25 night and said, I am the God of Abraham
your father. Do not be afraid, for I am with
you, and I will bless you and multiply
your seed for My servant Abraham's sake.
And he built an altar there and called
upon the name of Jehovah and pitched his
tent there. And there Isaac's servants dug
a well.

Date

Week 21 — Day 1   Today's verses

Gen. And Abraham gave all that he had to
25:5 Isaac.

26:12 And Isaac sowed in that land and gained
in the same year a hundredfold. And Jehovah blessed him.

Acts And with great power the apostles gave
4:33 testimony of the resurrection of the Lord
Jesus, and great grace was upon them all.

Date

Week 21 — Day 2   Today's verses

Gen. And when Abram was ninety-nine years
17:1 old, Jehovah appeared to Abram and said
to him, I am the All-sufficient God; walk
before Me, and be perfect.

18:14 Is anything too marvelous for Jehovah? At
the appointed time I will return to you, according to the time of life, and Sarah shall
have a son.

Date

Week 21 — Day 3   Today's verses

Gen. And the child grew and was weaned. And
21:8 Abraham made a great feast on the day
that Isaac was weaned.

Gal. The grace of our Lord Jesus Christ be with
6:18 your spirit, brothers. Amen.

1 Pet. As newborn babes, long for the guileless
2:2 milk of the word in order that by it you
may grow unto salvation.

Date

Week 22 — Day 4	Today's verses
Gen. 21:33	And Abraham planted a tamarisk tree in Beer-sheba, and there he called on the name of Jehovah, the Eternal God.
John 10:10	…I have come that they may have life and may have *it* abundantly.
6:57	As the living Father has sent Me and I live because of the Father, so he who eats Me, he also shall live because of Me.

Date _____

Week 22 — Day 5	Today's verses
Gen. 21:33	And Abraham planted a tamarisk tree in Beer-sheba, and there he called on the name of Jehovah, the Eternal God.
Psa. 90:2	…Indeed from eternity to eternity, You are God.
1 John 5:11	And this is the testimony, that God gave to us eternal life and this life is in His Son.

Date _____

Week 22 — Day 6	Today's verses
1 John 1:2	(And the life was manifested, and we have seen and testify and report to you the eternal life, which was with the Father and was manifested to us).
John 3:36	He who believes into the Son has eternal life; but he who disobeys the Son shall not see life…
Col. 3:4	When Christ our life is manifested, then you also will be manifested with Him in glory.

Date _____

Week 22 — Day 1	Today's verses
Rom. 8:4	That the righteous requirement of the law might be fulfilled in us, who do not walk according to the flesh but according to the spirit.
1 John 2:15	Do not love the world nor the things in the world. If anyone loves the world, love for the Father is not in him.

Date _____

Week 22 — Day 2	Today's verses
Gen. 21:30-32	And he said, These seven ewe lambs you shall take from my hand, that it may be a witness for me that I dug this well. Therefore he called that place Beer-sheba, because there the two of them swore an oath. So they made a covenant at Beer-sheba…
Luke 22:20	And similarly the cup after they had dined, saying, This cup is the new covenant established in My blood, which is being poured out for you.

Date _____

Week 22 — Day 3	Today's verses
Num. 21:17-18	Then Israel sang this song: Spring up, O well! Sing to it! The well, which the leaders sank, which the nobles of the people dug, with the scepter, with their staffs…

Date _____

Week 23 — Day 4

Today's verses

Heb. Counting that God was able to raise *men* 11:19 even from the dead, from which he also received him back in figure.

Rom. ...In the sight of God whom he believed, 4:17 who gives life to the dead and calls the things not being as being.

Date

Week 23 — Day 1

Today's verses

Gen. Now after these things God tested Abra-22:1-2 ham and said to him, Abraham. And he said, Here I am. And He said, Take now your son, your only son, whom you love, Isaac, and go to the land of Moriah, and offer him there as a burnt offering on one of the mountains of which I will tell you.

Date

Week 23 — Day 5

Today's verses

Gen. ...Because you have done this thing and 22:16-18 have not withheld your son, your only son, I will surely bless you and will greatly multiply your seed like the stars of the heavens and like the sand which is on the seashore; and your seed shall possess the gate of his enemies. And in your seed shall the nations of the earth shall be blessed...

Date

Week 23 — Day 2

Today's verses

Heb. By faith Abraham, being tested, offered 11:17 up Isaac; indeed he who gladly received the promises was offering up his only begotten.

Rom. Because out from Him and through Him 11:36 and to Him are all things. To Him be the glory forever. Amen.

Date

Week 23 — Day 6

Today's verses

Heb. But you have come forward to Mount 12:22-23 Zion and to the city of the living God, the heavenly Jerusalem; and to myriads of angels, to the universal gathering; and to the church of the firstborn, who have been enrolled in the heavens; and to God, the Judge of all; and to the spirits of righteous men who have been made perfect.

Date

Week 23 — Day 3

Today's verses

Gen. And Abraham called the name of that 22:14 place Jehovah-jireh, as it is said *to* this day, On the mount of Jehovah it will be provided.

Rev. And I saw, and behold, the Lamb standing 14:1 on Mount Zion, and with Him a hundred and forty-four thousand, having His name and the name of His Father written on their foreheads.

Date

Week 24 — Day 4   Today's verses

Gen. And Abraham said to his servant, the old-
24:2-4 est of his house, who ruled over all that he
had, Put your hand under my thigh; and I
will make you swear by Jehovah, the God
of heaven and the God of earth, that you
will not take a wife for my son from the
daughters of the Canaanites, among whom
I am dwelling. But you shall go to my
country and to my relatives, and take a
wife for my son Isaac.

Date

Week 24 — Day 5   Today's verses

Gen. And *food* was set before him to eat. But he
24:33 said, I will not eat until I have stated my
business. And he said, Speak on.

1 Pet. Chosen according to the foreknowledge of
1:2 God the Father in the sanctification of the
Spirit unto the obedience and sprinkling of
the blood of Jesus Christ…

Date

Week 24 — Day 6   Today's verses

Gen. And when the camels had finished drink-
24:22 ing, the man took a golden nose-ring weighing half a shekel and two bracelets for her
hands weighing ten gold shekels.

1 Pet. Whom having not seen, you love; into
1:8 whom though not seeing *Him* at present,
yet believing, you exult with joy *that is*
unspeakable and full of glory.

Date

Week 24 — Day 1   Today's verses

Gen. … You will not take a wife for my son from
24:3-4 the daughters of the Canaanites, among
whom I am dwelling. But you shall go to
my country and to my relatives, and take a
wife for my son Isaac.

22:17 I will surely bless you and will greatly
multiply your seed like the stars of the
heavens and like the sand which is on the
seashore; and your seed shall possess the
gate of his enemies.

Date

Week 24 — Day 2   Today's verses

Gen. And he said to me, Jehovah, before whom
24:40 I walk, will send His angel with you and
make your journey prosperous. And you
shall take a wife for my son from my family, even from my father's house.

48 And I bowed and worshipped Jehovah
and blessed Jehovah, the God of my master Abraham, who had led me in the right
way to take the daughter of my master's
brother for his son.

Date

Week 24 — Day 3   Today's verses

Gen. And the girl was very beautiful in appear-
24:16 ance, a virgin, and no man had known her.
And she went down to the spring and filled
her pitcher and came up.

20 And she hurried and emptied her pitcher
into the trough and ran again to the well
to draw *water*, and she drew *it* for all his
camels.

Date